DANIEL

FINDING CONFIDENCE *that* GOD'S POWER *is at* WORK

Written by Kayla Ferris and designed by Stephanie Norton

Copyright © 2024 by Proverbs 31 Ministries
All Scripture quotations are English Standard Version (ESV) unless otherwise noted.

WE MUST EXCHANGE WHISPERS *with* GOD BEFORE SHOUTS *with the* WORLD.
Lysa TerKeurst

Pair your study guide with the First 5 mobile app!

This study guide is designed to accompany your study of Scripture in the First 5 mobile app. You can use it as a standalone study or as an accompanying guide to the daily content within First 5.

First 5 is a free mobile app developed by Proverbs 31 Ministries to transform your daily time with God.

Go to the app store on your smartphone, download the First 5 app, and create a free account!

www.first5.org

WELCOME to the BOOK of
DANIEL

I had prayed. A lot. Yet my situation hadn't changed. *What's the point of even praying?* I thought. It wasn't so much that I questioned whether God *could* change my circumstances, but it didn't seem like He *would*. Where was He?

I wish I could say this was a one-time struggle. Yet I find myself back in this place over and over again. I wonder where God is. I wrestle with feeling like I'm not able to see Him moving. I question both His plan and His heart. If I'm being honest, sometimes I lack confidence that His power is at work in my life.

Yet here's the thing about confidence — it grows or shrinks depending on what you feed it. Confidence is gained through experience and repeated patterns: seeing something happen once, twice, three times, and therefore believing it can happen again. We develop confidence in things that do not change or shift but remain solid. All of this means **it is possible for us to grow in our confidence in God.**

Here is where the book of Daniel shines. Throughout our study of Daniel, we will witness God's power at work over and over again. He will rescue men from a fiery furnace and a den of lions. He will give His people wisdom and favor in the sight of kings. He will give visions of the future, and He will control empires. He will always have a plan and will always be in control. And seeing so many examples of God's power at work does so much good for my soul. Knowing that God never changes, that He is the same yesterday, today and forever (Hebrews 13:8), gives me a solid rock on which I can build confidence in Him.

And when I start to find confidence in God's power at work, something in me changes. I notice little things I didn't see before: evidences of God's goodness. I start to pray differently, trusting that God hears and knows — and not shying away from bold requests for Him to do the miraculous. I stop fretting about the world around me because it all fits into His great plan. I walk through life with my head held high, knowing my future, my eternity with Him, is guaranteed.

Yes, things change when we find confidence that God's power is at work not just in our own lives but in the world as a whole, throughout history, and into the future. And I know just the place you can go if you want to build that confidence …

Let's open our Bibles to the book of Daniel.

Kayla

WHO WROTE DANIEL *and* WHEN?

The traditional belief is that this book of the Bible was written by a sixth-century Jew named Daniel, who was taken captive along with many other Jews when God's people were exiled to Babylon. The first half of the book is written in third person, referring to Daniel as though he were not the narrator: e.g., "*But Daniel resolved that he would not defile himself ...*" (Daniel 1:8). Much of the second part of the book is written in first person, appearing to be narrated by Daniel himself: e.g., "*As for me, Daniel, my spirit within me was anxious ...*" (Daniel 7:15). This shifting point of view may be explained by the fact that it was common in the Ancient Near East for a co-writer or editor to oversee the writing of a manuscript while the main author dictated. If Daniel was the author, the writing took place between the first year of the Babylonian King Nebuchadnezzar's reign in 605 B.C. and the third year of Cyrus' reign in 536 B.C.

However, an alternate view has been suggested by some scholars. Because Daniel 11 is so detailed in its predictions about the second century, they suggest that it must have been written during the reign of Antiochus IV, sometime between 175-164 B.C. In other words, these scholars conclude that the prophecies were not written down until they had already been fulfilled. This idea of "prophecies after the fact" would suggest that someone wrote under the pseudonym "Daniel" to help give the people of the time some way to interpret the horrible circumstances they were going through.

Through human eyes, this view makes sense. However, the Bible tells us in Isaiah 44:6-7, "*Thus says the LORD, the King of Israel and his Redeemer, the LORD of hosts: 'I am the first and I am the last; besides me there is no god. Who is like me? Let him proclaim it. Let him declare and set it before me, since I appointed an ancient people.* **Let them declare what is to come, and what will happen**'" (emphasis added). No one is like God. He knows the future perfectly, down to every detail. Therefore, God could have given prophecies to Daniel in exact detail long before these events took place. In many instances throughout Scripture, God did precisely that: For instance, He gave the prophet Isaiah specific insight that the Messiah would be born of a virgin (Isaiah 7:14), which Jesus was some 700 years later (Luke 1:34-35).

Additionally, around 171-167 B.C., a group called the Qumran began to copy much of the Old Testament and stored these scrolls in caves. We now refer to these as the Dead Sea Scrolls. Fragments of eight manuscripts of Daniel (overall containing all 12 chapters) have been found among the Dead Sea Scrolls. It is difficult to believe the Qumran would have accepted a book that was just newly written into their canon, or their list of books officially accepted as genuine and God-inspired.

Throughout our study together, we will accept Daniel as the author and 605-536 B.C. as the approximate writing date, believing that God has the power to see and hold the future in His hand.

WHERE DOES DANIEL FIT *in the* BIBLICAL NARRATIVE?

In Genesis 12, God made a covenant with a man named Abram to *"make of [him] a great nation"* that would bless the world (v. 2). This nation eventually became known as Israel. When God called the Israelites out of Egyptian slavery (as recorded in Exodus), He made a renewed covenant with them: He would be their God, and they would be His chosen people to represent Him to the world. God would give them land, and He would go before them and look out for them.

They, in turn, were to follow His laws and commandments. God told them a crucial piece to this covenant in Leviticus 26, when He said increasing consequences would come *"if you [Israel] will not listen to me and will not do all these commandments, if you spurn my statutes, and if your soul abhors my rules, so that you will not do all my commandments, but break my covenant"* by living in sin (vv. 14-15). If the people still failed to listen and repent, God gave a final consequence: *"I will scatter you among the nations, and I will unsheathe the sword after you, and your land shall be a desolation, and your cities shall be a waste"* (Leviticus 26:33).

After leaving Egypt, the people of Israel then wandered in the wilderness but finally came into their promised land. God sustained them and gave them victories along the way. But as the people settled into the land, temptations

arose. The idols and gods of their enemies enticed them, and they fell into sin.

God sent a series of judges to bring the people back to Him — but they said they would rather have a king. Therefore, God established a line of kings, including Saul, David and Solomon. However, as the line of kings went on, the people pulled further and further away from God. God called them back. He sent prophets to warn them of the consequences of their sinful choices. But they would not listen. Their hearts were hard.

After years and years of the people not listening to God's calls to repentance, God issued the final consequence of the covenant He made with them long ago. The rising nation of Babylon came into Judea, and many of the Jewish people were captured and carried away to the city of Babylon. We learn in Daniel 1:1-6 that Daniel was among the captured, along with his friends Shadrach, Meshach and Abednego (also known as Hananiah, Mishael and Azariah). In 586 B.C. Babylon completely destroyed the city of Jerusalem, burning the temple of God along with it.

Yet back in Leviticus 26, God had not stopped His promises after saying His people would be carried away and their cities destroyed. The very end of Chapter 26 included this important detail: "*Yet for all that, when they are in the land of their enemies, I will not spurn them, neither will I abhor them so as to destroy them utterly and break my covenant with them, for I am the LORD their God. But I will for their sake remember the covenant with their forefathers, whom I brought out of the land of Egypt in the sight of the nations, that I might be their God: I am the LORD*" (vv. 44-45).

God would still be with His people, even when they were in a foreign land. He would still be their God. We can see the evidence of this promise all throughout the book of Daniel: God was with Daniel. He had a plan.

Daniel also illustrates for us that God's character, power and presence will always and forever be trustworthy. God is with us today. He is in control right now, and He has a plan for our future. We can believe in His faithfulness to see it through.

Introduction | 9

the BABYLONIAN EMPIRE

The book of Daniel begins with the line, *"In the third year of the reign of Jehoiakim king of Judah, Nebuchadnezzar king of Babylon came to Jerusalem and besieged it"* (Daniel 1:1). It was during this siege that some of the Jewish youth were brought back to Babylon to serve the king. This is how Daniel found himself in service to King Nebuchadnezzar in the city of Babylon, far from his home in Israel.

The Babylonian Empire that lasted from 626-539 B.C. is sometimes also referred to as the Neo-Babylonian Empire ("neo" meaning "new") because Babylon itself had existed long ago. Before 626 B.C., it was under Assyrian rule. But as the Assyrian Empire was crumbling under civil war, a man by the name of Nabopolassar rose up to claim the city of Babylon as the capital for the new kingdom of Babylon. He would pass on this kingdom to his son, Nebuchadnezzar II.

Under Nebuchadnezzar, the Babylonian Empire rose to become a major imperial power. Located 50 miles south of present-day Baghdad in Iraq, the city of Babylon became arguably the largest city in the world. The Euphrates River ran through the middle, and Nebuchadnezzar fortified the city by surrounding it with 40-foot-tall walls, which were so thick that ancient legends suggested chariot races were held on top. Babylon was the home of the alleged hanging gardens, thought to be one of the Seven Wonders of the World.

Two large and ornate palaces were also built there, as well as numerous temples dedicated to the many Babylonian gods. The largest of these temples was the ziggurat Etemenanki, dedicated to the god Marduk. This seven-layer building is believed to have been almost 300 feet tall. Along the walls of the city were a number of gates, with the most famous being the Ishtar Gate. Located near the king's palaces, it was built of blue glazed bricks and decorated with images of bulls and dragons. This opened up to the Processional Way, a half-mile corridor lined with images of lions, which led to the ziggurat Etemenanki. All of the building and construction of such a city took a major labor force, which Nebuchadnezzar created by forming labor gangs from the many surrounding lands he conquered. Bringing these people into the city also increased the diversity of the population.[1,2]

Nebuchadnezzar ruled the Babylonian Empire for 43 years. After his death, the empire sifted through the hands of a number of leaders and within 23 years was conquered by the rising empire of the Medo-Persians.

Despite its short life span, the Babylonian Empire, especially the city of Babylon, was a metropolitan region that was like nothing the world had yet seen. This was the city where Daniel spent most of his life, doing his best to stay faithful to the one true God.

the MEDO-PERSIAN EMPIRE

Partway through the book of Daniel, which begins in the Babylonian Empire (Daniel 1:1), we see a power shift as Babylon was overtaken: "*That very night Belshazzar the [Babylonian] king was killed. And Darius the Mede received the kingdom, being about sixty-two years old*" (Daniel 5:30-31). This marked the rise of the Medo-Persian Empire (so called because the Mede Empire was conquered and merged into the Persian Empire). Many historians also refer to this time period as the Achaemenid Empire.

The Medo-Persian Empire stretched from 559-331 B.C. In modern-day terms, Persia is often associated with Iran. But while ancient Persia did cover modern Iran, the empire of this time was much more expansive, stretching from Egypt in the west to parts of India and Pakistan to the east.

The first major king of the Medo-Persian Empire was Cyrus II, sometimes referred to as Cyrus the Great. Unlike many conquering kings before him, Cyrus was known for showing mercy toward those he conquered. He allowed regions to continue many of their local practices, traditions and religions. Particularly, we know the Persian Empire allowed Jewish exiles in Babylon to return to Jerusalem and rebuild the temple and city walls (Ezra 1:1-2; Nehemiah 2:7-8).

Cyrus, and later Darius, began to see that an empire as large as Persia needed structure. The empire was divided into 20 provinces with governors over each region. Road systems were built, postal and communication services were established, and coinage was created.

Daniel was an elderly man when he served briefly under the Persian King Cyrus. It's helpful to note that in Daniel 5:31-6:28, there are early references to "*Darius*," but this is not believed to be the later King Darius who ruled from 522-486 B.C. In this biblical context, "*Darius*" is often thought to be the Mede name for King Cyrus II. Many interpret Daniel 6:28 as technically saying, "*So this Daniel prospered during the reign of Darius, [that is], the reign of Cyrus the Persian.*"

Another book of the Bible, the book of Esther, also took place during the Persian Empire. The King Ahasuerus who is mentioned in the book of Esther is believed to be the same person as King Xerxes I. Historically, King Xerxes attempted to invade Greece but was quickly defeated. Doing so depleted the royal treasury, and the Persian Empire began to quickly decline until it was conquered by Alexander the Great in 334 B.C. Alexander's swift victory across the area marked the end of the Persian Empire and ushered in the Greek Empire.

GENRES *and* STRUCTURE *of* DANIEL

The book of Daniel can be broken up into two sections, both of which increase our confidence in God's power in different ways.

The first half of the book (Chapters 1-6) consists of what we call historical narrative. In these chapters, we will find six different true stories, all written in third person and recounted in chronological order.

These stories include:

- Nebuchadnezzar's dream of a statue made of different materials (Daniel 2).
- Three men thrown into a fiery furnace for not bowing to a golden idol (Daniel 3).
- Nebuchadnezzar's second dream and its fulfillment when he became like an animal living outside (Daniel 4).
- A mysterious hand that wrote on a wall (Daniel 5).
- Daniel miraculously surviving a den of lions (Daniel 6).

The second half of the book of Daniel (Chapters 7-12) consists of prophetic visions. Daniel witnessed four different visions from God and wrote them all down in first person.

The visions are also recorded in chronological order as they appeared to Daniel:

- Daniel's first vision: of four beasts (Daniel 7).
- His second vision: of a ram and a goat (Daniel 8).
- His third vision: of the angel Gabriel (Daniel 9).
- His final, and lengthiest, vision: of a terrifying man along with kings of the north and south (Daniel 10-12).

Daniel's visions are sometimes described as "apocalyptic," which comes from the Greek word *apokalypsis*, meaning "revelation." The apocalyptic visions of Daniel were to reveal something about the future. Apocalyptic literature is very symbolic in nature and often layered in its interpretations.

Also interesting about the book of Daniel is that it was written in multiple languages. Daniel 1-2:4a was written in Hebrew; then Daniel 2:4b-7:28 was all written in Aramaic. The book then switched back to Hebrew in Daniel 8-12. Scholars are not quite sure as to the reasoning behind the language changes, though some suggest perhaps the opening and ending were directed specifically toward the Jewish people while the rest of the book was meant to have a more widespread audience.

THEMES *and* PURPOSE *of* DANIEL

The stories and visions of Daniel, like all of God's Word, have the ability to speak to people of every generation. These words would have inspired hope for the people living in Babylonian exile during the days of Daniel. They would have been an anchor for the souls of people living during horrible persecution at the hands of Antiochus IV in the Greek Empire. And the people of God who lived during the later Roman Empire, who witnessed the destruction of Jerusalem and the temple (again) in A.D. 70, would have received courage and faith through the words of Daniel as well.

The same is true of us today, living *"in these last days"* before Jesus' second coming (Hebrews 1:2). Bible scholar Dale Davis calls the book of Daniel "a realistic survival manual for the saints."[1] As we live in this world, waiting for Christ to return, the themes of Daniel can guide us toward confidence in God's present and future power based on His past faithfulness.

Throughout the book of Daniel, we learn that:

- It is possible to remain faithful to God in an antagonistic world.

- God will humble the proud, and He will raise the humble. Therefore, we should strive for humility.

- Persecution is to be expected for God's people. We shouldn't be surprised by it, but we can trust that God is working even in painful seasons.

- No king or kingdom of this world is bigger than God. No matter how our circumstances look, God's power is at work and is greater than any other. God is sovereign over history and over hearts.

- As followers of God, we are part of a battle in the spiritual realms. But we do not walk in this alone.

- God knows the time for everything, and that includes the end of time. We can know for certain that one day, evil will end.

- God's Kingdom will last forever.

When we know these truths in both our heads and our hearts, we can have faith and hold on to Jesus no matter what comes our way!

MAJOR MOMENTS

Week One

DAY 1 *Daniel 1:1-7*
Daniel and other Hebrew youths were taken into exile in Babylon.

DAY 2 *Daniel 1:8-21*
Daniel and his three friends resolved not to eat the king's food.

DAY 3 *Daniel 2:1-16*
After his dream, Nebuchadnezzar created an impossible situation for his wise men.

DAY 4 *Daniel 2:17-30*
Daniel prayed and praised God for revealing the king's dream.

DAY 5 *Daniel 2:31-49*
The dream's interpretation displayed God's sovereignty over earthly kingdoms.

Week Two

DAY 6 *Daniel 3:1-7*
Nebuchadnezzar commanded all peoples to worship a golden image.

DAY 7 *Daniel 3:8-18*
Shadrach, Meshach and Abednego refused to worship the image.

DAY 8 *Daniel 3:19-30*
God delivered Shadrach, Meshach and Abednego from the fiery furnace.

DAY 9 *Daniel 4:1-18*
Nebuchadnezzar dreamed about a great tree being cut down.

DAY 10 *Daniel 4:19-27*
The dream foretold that Nebuchadnezzar would be humbled until he recognized that heaven rules.

Week Three

DAY 11 *Daniel 4:28-37*
Nebuchadnezzar was humbled and then restored.

DAY 12 *Daniel 5:1-12*
Belshazzar was frightened by a hand writing on the wall.

DAY 13 *Daniel 5:13-31*
Daniel interpreted the writing, predicting Belshazzar and Babylon's defeat.

DAY 14 *Daniel 6:1-9*
Darius signed a decree outlawing petitions to any god or man for 30 days.

DAY 15 *Daniel 6:10-18*
Daniel defied the king's decree and was thrown into the den of lions.

WEEK FOUR

DAY 16 *Daniel 6:19-28*
God shut the lions' mouths and saved Daniel.

DAY 17 *Daniel 7:1-8*
Daniel had a vision of four beasts.

DAY 18 *Daniel 7:9-14*
Daniel saw the Ancient of Days and one like a Son of Man.

DAY 19 *Daniel 7:15-28*
Daniel's vision of beasts was interpreted for him.

DAY 20 *Daniel 8:1-14*
Daniel had a vision of a ram being overthrown by a goat that grew an evil horn.

WEEK FIVE

DAY 21 *Daniel 8:15-27*
Daniel's vision of a ram and a goat was interpreted for him.

DAY 22 *Daniel 9:1-19*
Daniel prayed and made confession for himself and his people.

DAY 23 *Daniel 9:20-27*
The angel Gabriel answered Daniel's prayer with a vision of 70 weeks.

DAY 24 *Daniel 10:1-9*
Daniel's final vision began with a man.

DAY 25 *Daniel 10:10-21*
A heavenly messenger strengthened Daniel.

WEEK SIX

DAY 26 *Daniel 11:1-19*
A vision was given regarding the future kings of the south and north.

DAY 27 *Daniel 11:20-35*
The kings of the south and north continued in evil for an appointed time.

DAY 28 *Daniel 11:36-45*
The vision showed the king of the north growing in terror until the time of the end comes.

DAY 29 *Daniel 12:1-4*
The vision ended with a look at the devastation and resurrection to come.

DAY 30 *Daniel 12:5-13*
Daniel was told that the end would come and that, until then, he should go his way.

WEEK ONE

DANIEL 1:1-7
Daniel and other Hebrew youths were taken into exile in Babylon.

Sometimes the start of a great story needs a little backstory. Perhaps this is why the book of Daniel opens with a brief history lesson about the nation of Judah. Despite repeated warnings from God, Judah had continued in their pattern of sin. So God was faithful to carry out His covenant, and He allowed the nation to be conquered by Babylon.

The key word here is "allowed." God was orchestrating the events that took place. Nothing took God by surprise. And Daniel reminded his readers of this truth right from the start.

Daniel 1:2 tells us Babylon's King Nebuchadnezzar stole *"some of the vessels of the house of God"* and brought them into the *"treasury of his god."* This was Babylon's way of saying, "Our god is better and stronger than yours."

- However, what do the very first words of Daniel 1:2 remind us about who was actually in control here?

Daniel 1:4 continues by mentioning that some of Israel's youths (likely teenagers) were taken into exile and brought to Babylon. Teenagers have their entire lives before them. They have plans and goals and dreams. Yet for the four young men mentioned in Daniel 1:7, exciting plans for the future must have been shattered as they were forced to leave everything behind.

- When have things not gone according to your plan for your own life? What were your thoughts toward God in those moments?

Week One | 21

Bible scholar Dale Davis says, "Sometimes God may allow hardships to reach us because he wants his mercy to reach beyond us."[1] It might have been hard for these teenagers to see beyond their difficult circumstances, but through their exile, God was positioning them to shine His light into the heart of enemy territory. King Nebuchadnezzar thought he was *taking*, but God was strategically *placing*.

Proverbs 19:21 says, "*Many are the plans in the mind of a man, but it is the purpose of the* LORD *that will stand*." It is OK to make plans and set goals. But we also step back from our own ideas and remember God's purpose ultimately prevails.

- Read Isaiah 55:8-11. What do we learn about God's thoughts and His words? How does this truth help you when things don't go according to plan?

King Nebuchadnezzar's plan was to take Israel's top young people and have them contribute to his kingdom. Let's take a look at his tactics.

NEBUCHADNEZZAR'S TACTICS

ISOLATION	Daniel 1:3-4: "*... bring some of the people of Israel ... youths without blemish ...*"	By separating the youth from their homes, families, older generations, etc., Babylon ensured they would be more susceptible to influence.
INDOCTRINATION	Daniel 1:4: "*... teach them the literature and language of the Chaldeans.*"	They learned all about Babylonian (aka Chaldean) culture, including astrology, mythology and pagan deities. Also note that indoctrination has the greatest impact on the young.

INDULGENCE	Daniel 1:5a: *"The king assigned them a daily portion of the food that the king ate, and of the wine that he drank."*	These youths were completely immersed in Babylon's ways and enticed with luxury. In a way, the Babylonians were kind, and this made them seductive.
IDENTITY CONFUSION	Daniel 1:7: *"And the chief of the eunuchs gave them names …"*	Daniel's Hebrew name meant "God is my judge." Hananiah's name meant "Yahweh is gracious." Mishael's name meant "Who is like God?" Azariah's name meant "Yahweh helps." Their new Babylonian names referred to Babylonian gods, like Marduk, Bel and Nebo. They were to be stripped of their identity in God.

◉ How can you see some of these same tactics being used against young Christians today?

Like the Hebrew youths in Daniel, as followers of Christ, we, too, live in a foreign land. Our true citizenship is in heaven (Philippians 3:20). And this world we live in now is hostile toward our belief that salvation is found in Christ alone.

◉ Read Romans 12:2. What is one thing you can do today to take a stand against becoming conformed to the ways of this world?

DANIEL 1:8-21
*Daniel and his three friends resolved
not to eat the king's food.*

The world around us is always attempting to influence how we live. Yesterday we studied how King Nebuchadnezzar attempted to assimilate Daniel and other Hebrew youths into Babylonian culture. They were given new homes, new education, new food and new names. All they needed to do was go along with it — and become Babylonian.

- But according to Daniel 1:8, what was Daniel's reaction to the king's plan (and the reaction of his three friends, who supported him in verses 11-13)?

The ESV Bible uses the word "*resolved*" in Daniel 1:8. In the original Hebrew, there are actually three words used: *sum*, meaning "set"; *al*, meaning "upon"; and *lev*, meaning "heart." Daniel **set it upon his heart** that he would live differently.

Scholars have different ideas as to why Daniel refused the food and wine. It might have been because the food was ceremonially unclean (using ingredients like animal blood, fat or shellfish, which God's law declared inedible). However, wine was not prohibited by God's law, and Daniel still refused wine. It might also be that the food had first been offered to idols. However, the vegetables Daniel and his friends did eat (v. 12) probably also would have been offered to idols.

The most common theory is that Daniel and his friends were choosing to take a stand against complete assimilation. The food they ate was one way they could set themselves apart. It was a continual reminder for them that as God's people, they were called to be different.

As Christ followers, we, too, are set apart and called to be different. First Peter 2:9 says, "*But you are a chosen race, a royal priesthood, a holy nation, a people for his own possession.*"

- Continue reading in 1 Peter 2:11-12. According to these verses, in what ways are we similar to Daniel? What might it look like in your life to live set apart from the world?

The wisdom Daniel had, even in his youth, is compelling. He handled the situation with such care and humility. First, Daniel 1:8 says he "*asked*" (note that he didn't *demand*) for a different meal plan. Though the answer in verse 10 was kind and compassionate, it was still a no. Instead of giving up, throwing a fit or retaliating, Daniel found an alternative solution: the "*test*" described in verses 12-16.

- How do you typically handle tough situations? When you face opposition, are you more likely to give up, get angry or look for another solution? What can you learn by studying Daniel's approach?

We have spent a lot of time looking at Daniel today. But Daniel is ultimately not the star of this story.

- Read Daniel 1:9 and Daniel 1:17. What subtle phrases do you see in these verses about who was at work here?

We long to see God show up in powerful ways. Stories of God closing the mouths of lions and showing up to protect people in fiery furnaces (which we'll read in the coming weeks!) bolster our faith. But let's not forget that God is *always* working, moving, and showing up in powerful ways — they just don't always have big fanfare. Sometimes God moves quietly, behind the scenes, in ways so subtle that if we aren't paying attention, we just might miss them. But rest assured: God is always there.

- Where in your life do you long to see God show up in a powerful way? Take a moment to pray for His work and will to be done. Have faith that God is working, even if you can't see it right now.

DAY 3

DANIEL 2:1-16

After his dream, Nebuchadnezzar created an impossible situation for his wise men.

Daniel 1 has shown us that God was working through Daniel and his friends. Daniel 1:17 said God gave them learning and skill. Verse 20 said when it came to wisdom and understanding, they were 10 times better than all the magicians and enchanters in Babylon! All of that God-given wisdom was about to be put to use.

- In Daniel 2, King Nebuchadnezzar "*had dreams*" (v. 1). How did he feel about and respond to these dreams?

In the ancient world, dreams were regarded as significant because many believed the gods spoke to people and gave them predictions of future events through dreams. Archeologists have found tablets dating back to this time period that were used specifically for deciphering omens. In Babylon, a dream would be revealed to a diviner, who would then consult the Akkadian omen manuals to provide an interpretation. With this supposed newfound knowledge of the future, the person would then perform certain cultic rituals for protection.[1]

- Why do you think people have such a desire to know the future? What might be the danger in this desire?

The king's desire to know the future through his troubling dream made him desperate. And in Daniel 2:5-6, Nebuchadnezzar threw a curveball: He didn't just want his dream interpreted. He wanted the diviners to tell him what the dream was — without him describing it to them.

26 | Week One

The wise men of Babylon were cornered, and they knew it. They told the king in Daniel 2:10-11, *"There is not a man on earth who can meet the king's demand ... no one can show it to the king except the gods."* This was perhaps the most wise and true statement they ever made. There is a limit to human knowledge and wisdom. It can only take us so far. As 1 Corinthians 3:19a says, *"The wisdom of this world is folly with God."*

- Read Proverbs 2:6 and Psalm 111:10. What do we learn about true wisdom from these passages?

Requiring something from humans that can only come from God never works out. It created an impossible situation in Babylon. The wise men could not deliver what the king desired. The consequences also swept up Daniel and his friends in the dilemma; they were considered guilty by association (Daniel 2:12-13). The king's spirit would stay troubled. Daniel and his friends would die. It looked like a tragedy for everyone.

- Let's take a moment to compare how the people in Daniel 2 responded to the impossible situations they found themselves in. How and why was the unbeliever's response in Daniel 2:12 so different from the believer's response in Daniel 2:14-16?

- What might this remind us, as believers in God, about our impossible situations or worries about the future?

Scripture says Daniel *"replied with prudence and discretion"* (v. 14). What a statement! This type of response can only come from the wisdom, patience and peace given by God.

- Look up a definition for both "prudence" and "discretion." Then write a prayer asking the Lord to guide you in speaking and acting this way in some situation this week.

DAY 4

DANIEL 2:17-30
Daniel prayed and praised God for revealing the king's dream.

What is your go-to reaction when life gets hard? Do you complain, stress, hide under a pillow, panic? Babylon's wise men were in a hard situation: The king had asked them for something impossible by human standards. When they couldn't deliver, he wanted them destroyed. If there was any time for Daniel and his friends to panic, this was it. Yet today's reading teaches us an important truth about how we can react in troubling situations when we trust the power of God.

- In Daniel 2:17-18, what did Daniel tell his friends to do?

The answer to the question above is simple. But, friends, let's never forget it is also powerful! Prayer matters. Prayer reminds us to lift our eyes up to the place where our help comes from (Psalm 121:1). Prayer gives us access to and confidence in God's power. Prayer wasn't Daniel's last resort; it was his first response. It was the only thing Daniel could do that truly mattered. He didn't consult dream manuals or read liver guides as other ancient diviners did. He went to God.

And then he did something mind-blowing... He went to sleep (Daniel 2:19)! King Nebuchadnezzar hadn't slept a wink since his dream (v. 1), and here Daniel was, on the eve of his possible death, praying and simply going to bed. And God gave him a *"vision of the night"* (v. 19).

- How would you rate your confidence in God's power to answer your prayers? Do you pray but still worry? Do you pray but struggle to feel like it matters? Or do you pray and walk away from prayer with peace?

- We are all works in progress here. How might we increase our confidence and faith through prayer?

You might think that with his life on the line, Daniel would have been in a hurry to save not only himself but also his friends and co-workers after receiving his vision from God. But Daniel didn't run straight to the king of Babylon. He paused to address the King of both heaven and earth. Daniel praised God (vv. 20-23). Bible scholar Daniel Akin beautifully states: "Interpreting the dream [was] important, but knowing and worshiping God is ultimate."[1]

- Read Daniel's words of praise in Daniel 2:20-23. Write down attributes of God you find in these verses — then form your own words of praise based on what you observed.

Sometimes in life, the options before us look bleak. Sometimes we feel confused, wishing we knew what lay ahead. Sometimes we wait and wonder if things will ever change. Daniel 2:22 reminds us that God *"knows what is in the darkness."* The things we cannot see, God does. The future is crystal clear in God's eyes. Truly believing and trusting this truth will help us to step forward with wisdom and faith.

- Read James 1:5. Where in your life do you need to pray and praise God for wisdom?

Finally, Daniel was brought before the king (Daniel 2:24). But before he unveiled the dream and its meaning, before he saved his life and the lives of others, before he gave the king answers, Daniel wanted to make one thing very clear.

- Daniel 2:30 says the mystery was revealed — but not because of what? According to verse 28, who was truly responsible for the revelation? Why is this important?

Week One | 29

DANIEL 2:31-49
The dream's interpretation displayed God's sovereignty over earthly kingdoms.

At times, it takes a humbling experience to open our eyes to God's Truth. That's why God gave Nebuchadnezzar a dream that left the king troubled and desperate for answers. As we see God reveal the interpretation of the dream through Daniel in today's reading, we, too, will learn important truths about God's power at work.

Take a moment to look at the image titled "Nebuchadnezzar's Statue Dream" on Page 32. It is astonishing that the dream and interpretation would predict later historical events so accurately. In fact, it is so astonishing that it has caused some to say the book of Daniel could not have been written by Daniel during the Babylonian Empire and must have been composed in the second century B.C. This would suggest that God did not enable Daniel to foretell the future.

- But let's read Isaiah 46:10 and Job 14:5. How might these verses support the argument that the book of Daniel was written before the second century and the prophecies were real foretellings of future events?

There are other prophecies within the Bible that have also astonishingly come true. For instance: prophecies about the coming Messiah that were most certainly written centuries before Jesus' life on earth.

- Take a look at one such messianic prophecy in Psalm 2. In what ways are Psalm 2 and Daniel 2:31-35 similar?

We are reminded in Scripture that God is sovereign. He is over all earthly kingdoms. From presidents to dictators, regimes, democracies, nations, unions and alliances ... everything on earth will come and go. All except God's Kingdom. It is the only one that *"shall never be destroyed"* (Daniel 2:44).

After God revealed this truth through Daniel, King Nebuchadnezzar had an interesting reaction. On one hand, he praised God, telling Daniel, "*Your God is God of gods*" (v. 47). But the king also didn't try to get to know this God of gods. He didn't show any concern about what was coming after him. As one scholar notes, "Relieved that he was the head of gold ... he concerned himself with the present."[1]

- Romans 5:3-4 says we should "*rejoice in our sufferings*" because they produce endurance, character and hope. James 1:2-4 says we should "*count it all joy ... when [we] meet trials of various kinds*" because they produce steadfastness and maturity. With these scriptures and Nebuchadnezzar's pride in mind, what could be the spiritual danger in feeling too comfortable in life? How can we keep ourselves from becoming too comfortable?

The reminder of God's sovereignty over all earthly kingdoms was also for Daniel. Though the king now showered him with honors, gifts and promotions (Daniel 2:48), Daniel was still a young man of integrity who would not allow himself to be swayed by the lure of Babylonian culture. While he waited for God's eternal Kingdom to come, he would serve an earthly kingdom, as God allowed, for the time being (v. 49).

- Where have you been uniquely placed within your community, neighborhood, workplace or family? God has intentionally and sovereignly set you there. How can you serve there as you await the coming of God's forever Kingdom at Christ's return?

- Pastor and author Dr. David Jeremiah once said, "Since the whole world is in God's hands, your world is in God's hand."[2] How does this reminder give you confidence in God's power today?

Week One | 31

NEBUCHADNEZZAR'S STATUE DREAM

PARTS of the STATUE	WHAT the IMAGERY REPRESENTS	HISTORICAL FACTS
HEAD OF GOLD *(Daniel 2:32, 37-38)*	Babylon	Luxurious home of the fabled hanging gardens, thought to be one of the Seven Wonders of the World. Empire only lasted 65 years.
CHEST AND ARMS OF SILVER *(Daniel 2:32, 39)*	Medo-Persia	A vast empire that lasted over 200 years.
MIDDLE AND THIGHS OF BRONZE *(Daniel 2:32, 39)*	Greece	Famed Alexander the Great would conquer most of the known world at the time. He died at the young age of 33. Empire lasted 185 years.
LEGS OF IRON/ FEET OF IRON AND CLAY *(Daniel 2:33, 40-43)*	Rome	Considered to be one of history's greatest empires. Many of its influences carry on today. It was a vast empire, consisting of many nations and people groups who were forced to be united under the Roman government. Western Rome fell in A.D. 476.

The *"stone cut out by no human hand"* (Daniel 2:34) represents Christ, who is also described elsewhere in Scripture as a *"cornerstone"* (Psalm 118:22; Matthew 21:42; Acts 4:11), a stone of stumbling or a rock of offense (1 Peter 2:7-8; Romans 9:33; Isaiah 8:14). The role of the stone in Nebuchadnezzar's dream is most likely a picture of both Jesus' first and second comings (as most biblical and apocalyptic prophecies are multilayered).

WEEKEND REFLECTION *and* PRAYER

Let's take a look back at a few places where we saw God's power at work in this week's study:

First, Daniel 1:1-4 reminded us that exile was an opportunity in God's hands. God's people were placed in the middle of pagan peoples, and He would ultimately see to it that they would share the truth of the one true God.

The temptations of Babylon were hard to resist. Yet God gave His people incredible wisdom, favor and strength to stand apart and live differently for Him (Daniel 1:8-20).

Next, God gave Nebuchadnezzar a dream so upsetting that the king created an impossible situation for his wise men (Daniel 2:9-11). But God delights in humanly impossible situations because *all things are possible in Him.*

Daniel prayed and praised the God who knows what is in the darkness (Daniel 2:20-23). God sees deep and hidden things. His power is working even when human eyes cannot see it.

Then God laid out the future through the dream's interpretation (Daniel 2:31-45). He proved that He is in control of everything! He holds the future, the world, all the powers of the earth. We know without a doubt this is true because this future laid out in Daniel has become our history. God said it. It happened.

With God, challenges are opportunities, temptations can be turned away, the impossible becomes possible, the darkness is illuminated, and the future is planned. It was true then. It is still true for you today.

Father God, give us confidence in Your power at work. You are strong and mighty, and nothing is too difficult for You. We place our faith in You, knowing You are in control. You see, You hear, and You act in perfect and loving ways. We trust You today. In Jesus' name, amen.

NOTES

NOTES

WEEK TWO

DAY 6

DANIEL 3:1-7
Nebuchadnezzar commanded all peoples to worship a golden image.

When we left Chapter 2 of Daniel, King Nebuchadnezzar was telling Daniel, "*Truly, your God is God of gods and Lord of kings*" (v. 47). He then gave Daniel a high position in his government, and in turn, Daniel asked that his friends be promoted as well. It seems all was well in Babylon ... until we get to Chapter 3.

- King Nebuchadnezzar went from praising God one moment to doing what in Daniel 3:1? What specifically did he command in verses 4-6?

When the king praised God in Chapter 2, it appears he failed to learn an important truth — **God *alone* is worthy of worship.** He is not a god among other gods. He is the only One. Yet Nebuchadnezzar simply wanted to add God to his collection.

This is not so different from a false idea we see today: Some suggest whether you follow Buddha, Muhammad, Vishnu, Jesus or someone else, all religious paths will get you to the right place eventually. However, this is not what the Bible teaches. God established in the first two of His Ten Commandments that He alone is God (Exodus 20:1-4). Jesus, who is God (Titus 2:13; Philippians 2:5-8; Colossians 2:9), also said in John 14:6 that He alone is the way, the truth and the life.

Nebuchadnezzar's impulse to add God to his list of gods was a common but wrong idea. As Bible scholar Matthew Henry put it, "Idolaters are fond of novelty and variety. *They choose new gods.* Those that have many will wish to have more."[1] That is the thing with idols — they never fulfill us. They are never enough. We get bored and need more.

- An idol is anything we love, serve, need, long for, worship or look to as though it were equal with God or greater than God. Today's idols don't often look like golden statues, as we see here in Daniel. But remember: Even a good thing, if it becomes a god-thing, can be an idol. What might be some idols in today's culture?

Some idols are blatantly obvious. Others are a little more sneaky. But what they all have in common is a pressure to try to make us conform to false beliefs. Daniel 3 demonstrates several forms this pressure can take.

One form is through people. That might look like pressure from authority figures: For instance, the phrase "*King Nebuchadnezzar*" is used six times in today's reading, emphasizing that the order for idol worship came straight from the top guy. It is difficult to say "no" to the boss. Also notice the important people who were called to support this initiative (Daniel 3:2-3). These were the movers and shakers of that time. The influencers added to the pressure. These were also Daniel, Shadrach, Meshach and Abednego's co-workers, so to speak, in the Babylonian government. Talk about peer pressure!

- Where have you felt pressure from people to act, think or believe a certain way? (These could be good or bad ways.) What does Proverbs 12:26 remind us?

Nebuchadnezzar also used psychological pressure to get people to conform to his idea. We see part of this in the list of instruments in Daniel 3:5. This was like a grand orchestra, likely creating moving and emotional music. Pressure to conform increases when emotions are manipulated.

And what a strong emotion is fear! Nebuchadnezzar also used threats of death by fire, just in case the people weren't convinced (v. 6).

- In what ways do you see the world today trying to prey on people's emotions to promote false beliefs? How can we guard our hearts against this and remain true to God?

- Romans 12:3 tells us to think of ourselves with "*sober judgment*." How do you think you would react in the type of situation we see in Daniel 3:1-7? Why do you think this, and why might it be helpful to know this about yourself?

Week 2

DAY 7

DANIEL 3:8-18
Shadrach, Meshach and Abednego
refused to worship the image.

Hurt happens to all of us. Sometimes we get overlooked or pushed aside. Maybe someone comes along who is smarter, prettier or younger, and we feel forgotten. Maybe we see someone else rising in success, climbing the ladder, living the life we wish we had. Jealousy is a sneaky, dangerous hook that can catch us so easily. But the last thing we want is to be caught up in the sins of envy and bitterness.

Yesterday we studied how King Nebuchadnezzar created a golden image for everyone to worship. Today Daniel 3:8 starts out by saying concerned "*Chaldeans*" (likely referring to some of the astrologers and wise men of Babylon) came forward and "*maliciously accused*" the Jews. This phrase literally meant "to eat or devour."[1] This was vicious.

Such strong feelings had to originate somewhere ... We might recall Daniel 2:49, which says three young Jewish men were appointed to high positions. We get the sense that perhaps the Chaldeans were jealous. They had been overlooked or pushed aside. That hurt, left to fester and grow, had turned into an ugly bitterness that was ready to bite back.

- What might it look like to find confidence in God's power to heal your hurt, unhook your heart from jealousy, and give you freedom in His love? Or if you're currently living in that confidence, how does it feel, and how can you thank God?

Shadrach, Meshach and Abednego were accused. The king was furious, saying to them, "*And who is the god who will deliver you out of my hands?*" (Daniel 3:15c). Shadrach, Meshach and Abednego knew the answer. They replied, "*Our God whom we serve is able*" (v. 17).

Choose a few of the following verses to look up, and write down what you learn about what God is able to do:

- Ephesians 3:20:

- 2 Corinthians 9:8:

- Hebrews 7:25:

- Jude 1:24:

- Luke 1:37:

God once said to the prophet Jeremiah, "*Is anything too hard for me?*" (Jeremiah 32:27b). God's power is capable of handling any and every situation. Nothing can stand against Him. Whatever you are facing, God is able. You can go to Him in confidence and pray to Him, believing He has the power to fix all things.

- Where in your life do you most need to pray for God's power? Believe He is able. Consider taking a moment to pray right now.

The first words of Daniel 3:18 are powerful. The three men said, "*But if not ...*"

They knew God was able to save their lives. What they didn't know was *how* God would work out His plan. And get this — they would trust Him even if His plan was *not* to save their lives. What a statement! They were not focused so much on their deliverance as they were focused on obedience. There was nothing they wanted more than to serve and love God. Not safety, health, comfort — not even life. They wanted nothing more than Him. The Apostle Paul in the New Testament would later echo this sentiment: "*For to me to live is Christ, and to die is gain*" (Philippians 1:21).

- What might it look like for you to live focused on obedience to God even more than deliverance from earthly trials?

- The power in this passage is not that Shadrach, Meshach and Abednego had such faith. The power is in the fact that we serve such a great God. He is worthy of our sacrifice. Write a quick prayer of praise to God, declaring Him worthy and wonderful. Pray confidently for His power, obey in faith, and know you can leave the "how" in His hands.

DANIEL 3:19-30
God delivered Shadrach, Meshach and Abednego from the fiery furnace.

DAY 8

To stand up in bold faith is not easy. Occasionally it might even land us in heated situations — which happened literally for Shadrach, Meshach and Abednego. They had refused the king's order to worship a golden image. They believed in God's ability to deliver them but were also willing to die for their faith.

In today's reading, we find a furious Nebuchadnezzar heating the furnace as hot as it could possibly get, binding the men so they couldn't resist or fight back. Their cloaks, tunics and hats even added extra fuel to the fire (Daniel 3:19-21). Nebuchadnezzar wanted to make sure it was humanly impossible for them to survive — yet we have learned in the course of our study together that there is no impossible situation for God.

We may wonder if Shadrach, Meshach and Abednego started praying for the fire to go out or for the king to change his mind. God could have made that happen. Yet Daniel 3:23 says the three men *"fell bound into the burning fiery furnace."* The fire still came. God did not keep them out of the furnace.

- What did God do instead, according to Daniel 3:24-25?

God does not always shield us from hardship. Today, we still face difficult situations and troubles. But when we do, God promises He will not forsake His people (Hebrews 13:5). He will walk with us through it. We will not be alone.

- Read the words of Isaiah 43:1-2. What waters, rivers or fires are you facing right now? What does the Lord say to you in Isaiah 43:2?

Some scholars believe the fourth man in the furnace, described as being *"like a son of the gods"* in Daniel 3:25, was some kind of angel. Others suggest this was a theophany, or a manifestation of God's presence. Still others believe this was a Christophany, or a physical appearance of Christ before He lived on earth as a human. Either way, the truth remains that God provides us with divine help. No matter what we are going through, God is there too. He sees us and He cares.

In Daniel 3:26, when Nebuchadnezzar called Shadrach, Meshach and Abednego out of the furnace, the miracle was confirmed. Not a hair had been singed. Not a fiber of clothing burned. Not even the smell of smoke was on them. What a testimony to the *entirety* of God's protection over them. God's power covered them completely.

As we marvel at this amazing miracle, it is also important to remember that any miracle we witness on earth is just a taste of the feast that is to come in eternity.[1] Eventually Shadrach, Meshach and Abednego would die. Even the physical miracles Jesus performed in His earthly lifetime were temporary. The thousands He miraculously fed were eventually hungry again. Those He healed would eventually see a grave. However, a day is coming when God's people will live an **eternal miracle**. One day there will be no more death, mourning, crying or pain, and we will be in God's presence forever and ever (Revelation 21:1-4). If we give our lives to Jesus, He promises that miracle for us.

- How does the future miracle you will experience with Christ in eternity give you hope and confidence today?

While we await this perfect future with Christ, God also has not forgotten about us here and now! Ephesians 1 tells of many blessings God gives us today from *"heavenly places"* (Ephesians 1:3), including redemption, forgiveness, grace and wisdom.

- Read Ephesians 1:3-14. What other blessings from heavenly places are we given here on earth?

After he witnessed a miracle, Nebuchadnezzar praised *"the God of Shadrach, Meshach, and Abednego"* and even decreed blasphemy against God to be illegal in his empire (Daniel 3:28-29) ... but he didn't claim God as the Lord of his own life. He apparently didn't desire to learn more. He admired and respected the three men saved from his furnace, but he didn't follow their example of faith.

- How much like Nebuchadnezzar we all can be! We often acknowledge God is real yet hesitate to follow Him fully in *every* area of our lives. To end today's study, let's write a prayer asking God to help us desire Him more fully and deeply, with a heart that is genuine and motives that are pure (Psalm 139:23-24).

DAY 9

DANIEL 4:1-18
Nebuchadnezzar dreamed about a great tree being cut down.

Do you ever find yourself falling back into similar situations, repeating the same response yet expecting something different to happen? Interestingly, Daniel 4 has many similarities to Daniel 2. In both cases, King Nebuchanezzar had a dream that frightened him. Both times, his group of wise men could not give the king the interpretation he needed to hear. And both chapters tell us Daniel, a man filled with the Spirit of God, came forward with the truth only God could provide.

Unique to Chapter 4, however, is that it is written from Nebuchadnezzar's point of view. Also unique is that it starts with the ending in mind. Let's take a look ...

After Daniel previously interpreted Nebuchadnezzar's first dream, the story ended with the king falling on his face and paying homage to **Daniel**. He then said, *"Truly, your God is God of gods"* (Daniel 2:47, emphasis added).

- But by the end of this next dream, Nebuchadnezzar's words and actions will have changed. Again, we're beginning today's story with the end in mind: What differences do you notice between the way the king spoke after his first dream (Daniel 2:47) versus after his second dream (Daniel 4:1-3)?

We saw Nebuchadnezzar's reaction to his first dream, which was about a statue — namely, it seemed as if he were relieved to be the head of gold. We then watched him build a golden image and demand that everyone worship it. We saw his anger when anyone dared defy his word. Then when God showed up, he was moved to outlaw blasphemy against the God of Shadrach, Meshach and Abednego. Yet even in Daniel 4:4, we get a sense that stubborn pride remained in Nebuchadnezzar's heart when he was *"at ease in [his] house and prospering in [his] palace."*

- Scripture tells us what we can expect to come next in this story. What do we learn from Proverbs 16:18 and Proverbs 18:12?

Nebuchadnezzar went on to describe his next dream, which was of a great and mighty tree being cut down and the stump (characterized as a man in Daniel 4:16) becoming like an animal. Certainly something that seemed great was about to fall. And just like with the first dream, the king called his group of wise men. And just like the first time, they couldn't help him (vv. 6-7).

- There's a saying that "insanity is doing the same thing over and over again and expecting different results." Think of a time when you repeated the same mistake, expecting different results. Why do you think we do this? What can we do differently in the future to turn to God instead?

Nebuchadnezzar was relieved when Daniel came in "*at last*" (v. 8). The king knew Daniel could help him because, as he said to Daniel, "*You are able, for the spirit of the holy gods is in you*" (v. 18). Nebuchadnezzar was a pagan king, but even he could sense the true Spirit of God at work in someone's life.

- In the same way, unbelievers today should see something different in those who follow Jesus. What does Matthew 5:14-16 remind us?

- If you have accepted Jesus, then the power of God's Spirit is at work **in you**. What external evidence of this internal work can you (and others) see in your life? (See Galatians 5:22-25 for the fruit of the Spirit.)

DAY 10

DANIEL 4:19-27
The dream foretold that Nebuchadnezzar would be humbled until he recognized that heaven rules.

No one wants to be the bearer of bad news. Yet sometimes delivering hard truths is the most loving thing we can do for a person. In yesterday's reading, King Nebuchadnezzar talked about a great tree he had seen in a dream. This tree was cut down, and the stump was left to become like an animal. When Daniel arrived to interpret the dream's meaning, Daniel 4:19 says he was *"dismayed for a while, and his thoughts alarmed him."* He knew that the message was against the king and that it would be hard to hear.

- While Daniel may have worried about the king's reaction, the king assured him to continue with the interpretation. How is this similar to the wisdom we find in Proverbs 27:6?

- What godly friends in your life do you trust to be honest with you even if it's hard? Or how could you pray for God to help you find these friends?

Daniel was the bearer of bad news. The tree in the dream was the king. Nebuchadnezzar's greatness would be taken away from him, as would his mental faculties. He would become like an animal, living outside and eating grass. Today this kind of behavior is known as a rare psychological disorder called boanthropy.

This was a difficult message to deliver to this powerful ruler. We can learn a lot from studying *how* Daniel delivered this message.

DANIEL SPOKE WITH ...		
COMPASSION	Daniel 4:19	He spoke gently, wishing only good for the king.
CANDOR	Daniel 4:25	He spoke honestly, not backing away from the hard truth.
COUNSEL	Daniel 4:27	He had the answer that the king couldn't yet see: repentance. And he graciously shared that advice.

- In what situation in your life do you need God's help to speak with compassion, candor and counsel? Why is it important that we cover hard conversations in prayer and ground them in God's Truth?

Daniel 4:25 reminds us *"the Most High rules the kingdom of men and gives it to whom he will."* It is a message Nebuchadnezzar needed, and it is a message we need constantly as well. **Only God is great.** As the Amplified Bible says in Philippians 2:13, *"For it is [not your strength, but it is] God who is effectively at work in you, both to will and to work [that is, strengthening, energizing, and creating in you the longing and the ability to fulfill your purpose] for His good pleasure."*

- Believing that only God is great means we don't rely on our own strength. How is this both humbling and freeing?

Week 2 | 49

Inspired by Daniel 4:26, author Nancy DeMoss Wolgemuth made "*Heaven rules*" her life motto. She writes, "I try to keep a constant reminder that 'Heaven rules' in front of me all the time. As I watch the evening news ... When I got the diagnosis of my husband's cancer ... When I start to worry about the unknowns and what-ifs ... at the end of the day, I keep coming back to 'Heaven rules.'"[1]

- How does it give you confidence in life to know that heaven rules? In what ways can you keep this reminder before you?

Daniel ended the dream interpretation with some advice to Nebuchadnezzar: "*Break off your sins*" (Daniel 4:27). It was a loving reminder about repentance before God. Daniel knew if the king would turn from his pride, a better life awaited him.

- Let's end today's study by reading Acts 3:19-20. Sit with these verses for a few minutes. Ask God to reveal any areas where He is lovingly leading you to repentance.

WEEKEND REFLECTION *and* PRAYER

Let's take a look at where we saw God's power at work in this week's study:

First, Nebuchadnezzar created a golden image to showcase his kingly power (Daniel 3:1-6), but there is no man or earthly power that can even come close to the power of God.

Next, their confidence in God's power was so strong that Shadrach, Meshach and Abednego refused to love anything more than God. That included their own safety (Daniel 3:17-18).

When faced with a dangerous, impossible situation, Shadrach, Meshach and Abednego were not alone. God was with them in the middle of it (Daniel 3:25).

Lastly, Nebuchadnezzar's dream of the mighty tree being cut down showed that the things of this world will come and go … but there is one thing that stays the same. Over everything, heaven rules (Daniel 4:26).

Nothing can compare to God. When we begin to see and believe in His power at work in our lives, everything else pales in comparison. We won't be satisfied with what the world has to offer. We know that all of these temporary comings and goings are just a small part of the bigger picture, the bigger Kingdom of God. He sits on the throne in heaven and at the same time, as only He can, walks us through the trials of earth.

Almighty God, give us confidence in Your power at work. Nothing comes close to rivaling You. You are all we want and all we need. Thank You that You are always with us. We declare today, over everything that happens in our lives, that You, God, reign forever. In Jesus' name, amen.

NOTES

NOTES

WEEK THREE

DANIEL 4:28-37
Nebuchadnezzar was humbled and then restored.

DAY 11

There is a saying: Don't put off until tomorrow what can be done today. This is especially true when it comes to confronting our sin. In Daniel 4, Nebuchadnezzar had a dream warning that the king's sin of pride would be his downfall. Daniel offered him wise counsel: Repent before it's too late! And then a year passed where seemingly nothing happened. Did the king repent?

Today's reading shows he did not.

In Daniel 4:30, the king looked at his kingdom and bragged about what **he** had built by **his** mighty power for the glory of **his** majesty. Nebuchadnezzar had a very high opinion of himself. He thought of himself as a truly great man.

- What advice does Jesus give about being *"great"* in Matthew 20:25-28?

Theologian Charles Spurgeon once said, "The best man in the church is the man who is willing to be a doormat for all to wipe their boots on, the brother who does not mind what happens to him at all—so long as God is glorified."[1] This doormat analogy isn't perfect (it should *not* be taken to the extreme of justifying abuse or mistreatment, for instance), but it offers a memorable example of humility: lowering ourselves so God is exalted.

This is the opposite of how Nebuchadnezzar was living. And just as God had promised, Nebuchadnezzar's pride led to his humbling. He went from thinking he was the greatest human alive (Daniel 4:30) to acting subhuman (vv. 32-33). But this devastating blow was also a divine catalyst that seemingly changed Nebuchadnezzar's life. When Nebuchadnezzar recognized the truth of who was truly mighty, powerful and in control, he lifted his eyes to heaven, and his reason returned to him (v. 34).

- What did Nebuchadnezzar do as soon as his reason returned to him in verses 34-35?

- Therefore, we might say that all people who are responding reasonably to God should be doing what? How has this been your response?

Nebuchadnezzar said about God in verse 35, "*None can stay his hand or say to him, 'What have you done?'*" We are all tempted to question God sometimes. Maybe our question is, *God, how could You allow this?* It can be so difficult to understand God's will and ways when circumstances hurt so much. Yet we are learning through the book of Daniel that God is everlasting, and He sees the big picture — the eternal picture. While it's not easy, we can have faith that what is happening now is working for the good of that bigger picture.

- God hates suffering and pain. He has a plan to take it all away someday. How does knowing that God sees the big picture and has a plan for eternity help you through hard moments today?

Not only was Nebuchadnezzar's reason returned to him but also his "*majesty and splendor,*" his "*greatness*" and his kingdom (v. 36). But the emphasis here is on the word "*returned.*" If something could be returned (by God), that means it could be taken away (by God) — because it all belongs to God. This is true of anything we possess on this earth: our money, talents, family, health, even our minds. God is sovereign over all of these things, and that means even if they leave us, we still have the hope of heaven, a perfect eternity with God that will not be taken away if we trust in Jesus.

- Hold your hands out in front of you, palms up. This is what we have to offer God ... empty hands. This is what we brought with us into this world, and this is what we will leave with. Now imagine your empty hands grabbing hold of Jesus' hand in eternity. How does this make you feel about the temporary things of this world?

Scholars can't seem to agree if Nebuchadnezzar became a true follower of God. Only God knows the heart of a person. But whether we will meet this king in heaven one day or not, we can learn from his last words recorded in the book of Daniel (v. 37).

- Read all the last recorded words of Nebuchadnezzar in Daniel 6:37. If this next sentence you write were to become your last words, what would you want to say to the world?

LINE of BABYLONIAN KINGS

NEBUCHADNEZZAR
605-562 B.C.
Defeated Jerusalem, brought Jewish captives back to Babylon. Reigned for 43 years.

EVIL-MERODACH
562-560 B.C.
Son of Nebuchadnezzar. Assassinated by his brother-in-law Neriglissar.

NERIGLISSAR
560-556 B.C.
Ruled four years.

LABASHI-MARDUK
556 B.C.
Son of Neriglissar. Became king as a young boy but was murdered within a month.

NABONIDUS
556-539 B.C.
Conspirator in the assassination of Labashi-Marduk. Gained the throne but was sent 500 miles away on a "religious matter." Co-regent with his son Belshazzar.

BELSHAZZAR
550-539 B.C.
Son of, and co-regent with, Nabonidus. Acted as king in Babylon in his father's absence. Belshazzar is considered the last king of Babylon, as he was killed when the Medo-Persians invaded the city. (Notice Belshazzar's rule began only 12 years after the end of Nebuchadnezzar's rule.)

DANIEL 5:1-12
Belshazzar was frightened by a hand writing on the wall.

DAY 12

As we leave Daniel 4, Chapter 5 may feel like an abrupt jump. We are introduced to King Belshazzar (not to be confused with *Daniel's* Babylonian name, Belteshazzar — though notably, both names mean "Bel protect the king" or "Bel protect his life," Bel being a Babylonian god). Daniel 5:2 says Nebuchadnezzar was the Babylonian king Belshazzar's "*father*." However, the Aramaic word translated in English as "father" can also mean "ancestor" or "predecessor."

See the "**Line of Babylonian Kings**" on Page 58 for a more in-depth look at the kings' succession, but here's the bottom line: After Nebuchadnezzar died, it took less than 25 years for the entire Babylonian kingdom to be lost under Belshazzar's rule. History shows just how fickle is the quest for wealth and power.

- Take a moment to read Jesus' parable told in Luke 12:16-21. How might this relate to Belshazzar's feast in Daniel 5:1-4?

To add a little historical context to this story, the Medo-Persians were probably encamped outside Babylon's city walls during Belshazzar's feast. Granted, the walls were thought to be impenetrable, with legends suggesting they were so thick that a chariot pulled by four horses could ride on top of them, so Belshazzar didn't seem worried. Instead, he decided to bring out the vessels that had been stolen from the temple of Jerusalem. It was a show of power. It was a way of saying, "See, our gods are strong. Look who we defeated before!"

Yet Galatians 6:7 reminds us, "*Do not be deceived: God is not mocked.*"

When a human hand supernaturally appeared and wrote on the palace walls, to say King Belshazzar was frightened is an understatement (Daniel 5:5-6). Bible scholar Dale Davis points out that the phrase "*his limbs gave way*" in verse 6 can also be translated as "the knots of his loins were loosed" ... meaning this might refer to losing control of his bladder or bowels.[1] In his fear, the king called for the wise men of Babylon. He offered them money and power if they could interpret the handwriting. But the wise men of the day struck out again (vv. 7-8).

- What does 1 Corinthians 1:25 tell us about human knowledge? And what does wisdom from heaven look like? (See James 3:17.)

Daniel 5:10 says "*the queen*" then came in and spoke up. Most scholars agree this refers to the "queen mother," meaning Belshazzar's mother, Nitocris. History tells us Nitocris was the daughter of Nebuchadnezzar, and she aided in the ongoing construction of canals and bridges in Babylon after her father's death.[2] Here in Daniel 5, she stepped in, took control of a spiraling situation, and spoke reason (vv. 11-12).

- While we can only speculate, how do you think the events we have studied in her father's life may have impacted her at this moment?

At this point in the story, Daniel was in his 80s. Perhaps he was retired, or maybe he'd been demoted as new rulers came into power. Either way, God wasn't finished with Daniel.

- Is there anything in your life that you think exempts you from being a part of God's bigger plan? How does the story of Daniel remind you, young or old, that nothing deters God's power at work in your life?

The queen spoke great words about Daniel. But this moment was so much bigger than Daniel.

- Highlight the descriptions of Daniel in verses 11-12. The real truth of the matter is that **gifts reflect the Giver**. In what ways do these words actually describe God?

DAY 13

DANIEL 5:13-31
Daniel interpreted the writing, predicting Belshazzar and Babylon's defeat.

Sometimes when we face challenges, we want quick and easy answers. We are more interested in making the problem go away than we are in seeing what it has to teach us. But as was the case for King Belshazzar of Babylon, there are times when we need a lesson more than a solution.

In Daniel 5:13, Daniel was summoned. Belshazzar added an insult into the exchange, calling him *"that Daniel, one of the exiles of Judah, whom the king my father brought from Judah"* (v. 13). He acknowledged Daniel's reputation (v. 14) but tried to buy the answer from him (v. 16). We also notice that all Belshazzar wanted was for Daniel to *"read this writing and make known to [him] its interpretation"* (v. 15). However, Daniel had different plans. What was first needed was a history lesson.

- Philosopher George Santayana is credited with the now common saying, "Those who cannot remember the past are condemned to repeat it."[1] Why might Belshazzar have needed the history lesson Daniel gave him in verses 18-21?

- Why is it important that we study the past, especially the stories of people in the Bible?

Daniel 5:22 is a heartbreaking line. Belshazzar *"knew all this"* history. He had all of the facts and information and examples of how pride led to God's judgment, yet he refused to change. Knowledge itself is not enough.

- What does James 1:22-25 say? How do these verses give us a clue as to the difference between mere knowledge and true wisdom, especially when it comes to knowledge about God?

The phrase on the wall in Daniel 5:25 related to Aramaic weights (a mina, a shekel, and a half-shekel) and was also a play on words: If read as verbs, *"Mene, Mene, Tekel, and Parsin"* meant "Numbered, Numbered, Weighed and Divided." Belshazzar's days were numbered. In this case, he had only hours (v. 30). The time for judgment, symbolized by the references to scales and weights, was close at hand.

Years earlier, God had given His prophets foreknowledge of how the Babylonian Empire would conclude: Isaiah said the end would come quickly, while the people were preparing tables and eating and drinking (Isaiah 21:3-5; Isaiah 21:9). This is also a foreshadowing of things to come, when Christ will return and a time for judgment will arrive suddenly again.

- Read 1 Thessalonians 5:2-4 and 2 Peter 3:10. How does this remind you of today's passage in Daniel? What can we learn from these accounts?

Historians say instead of ramming the walls or gates of Babylon, the Medo-Persian army diverted water from the Euphrates River, which ran under the walls, into a nearby marsh. When the river was low enough, the soldiers simply waded under the walls and into the city from October 11-12 in 539 B.C. *"That very night, Belshazzar the Chaldean king was killed"* (Daniel 5:30).

There is no mention of repentance on Belshazzar's part. He heard the words of God's prophet, but as far as we know, he didn't allow them to change him. Bible scholar Dale Davis makes this personal when he writes, "When truth does not humble us or lead us to worship, we are simply Belshazzar clones."[2]

- Take a moment to ask the Spirit of God to cause the Word of God to come alive in you and change your heart. What is one truth from today's Scripture study you can put into action, letting your heart and mind be transformed?

DANIEL 6:1-9
Darius signed a decree outlawing petitions to any god or man for 30 days.

DAY 14

Some say the more things change, the more they stay the same. In other words, despite what looks like change on the outside, certain fundamental characteristics remain constant. In Daniel 6, we will see a change in empires — Babylon was captured, and the Medo-Persian reign had begun — but the same evil tactics were still being employed.

In Daniel 5:31 and again here in Daniel 6, we see a reference to the new emperor, Darius. While we have no other historical record of a Darius during this time, some scholars suggest Darius the Mede and Cyrus the Persian are one and the same. Others argue that Darius was Cyrus' general, Gabaru (or Ugbaru). Either way, in Daniel 6, Darius was now in charge.

In his empire, he established three officials over 120 satraps (provincial rulers in charge of security and collecting tribute from the people). The officials were to watch the satraps and make sure the king would *"suffer no loss"* (v. 2), meaning he wouldn't be cheated out of any money.

Corruption within the government isn't new. However, there was one standout official: Daniel. One scholar jokingly says Daniel 6 begins with a miracle: a squeaky-clean politician.[1] During the Babylonian Empire, Daniel and his friends had stood out. Now in the Medo-Persian Empire, Daniel stood out again.

- Do you think a person of God stands out in a government position today? Why or why not?

Daniel was said to have *"an excellent spirit"* in him (v. 3). This was the Spirit of God. While the Holy Spirit had not yet been sent to dwell in the hearts of all believers like He would be after the ministry of Jesus (John 7:39), the special way the Spirit filled Daniel is one of several examples in the Old Testament that serve as a foretaste of what was to come (e.g., Exodus 31:1-3; Genesis 41:38).

- If you are a follower of Jesus, you have God's excellent Spirit within you. What evidence of the Holy Spirit do you see in your life? How does it give you confidence to know that the Spirit of God is within you (Romans 5:5; Romans 8:11-16)?

Daniel had gone from the bottom to the top of his society, then back down and back up again. This was the second time Daniel found favor with a king — but both times, it proved to be costly. The first time almost cost his friends' lives (Daniel 3:19). This next promotion would almost cost his own life when the king issued an edict Daniel would not obey: a law forbidding prayer directly to God (Daniel 6:7-9).

- The Apostle Paul would later write about being content in all circumstances in Philippians 4:11-13. Let's think about this in terms of Daniel: What had he learned about contentment, whether he was living in the favor of worldly kings or not?

Sometimes success multiplies enemies. Whether they were jealous of his promotion, antisemitic, or just angry he wouldn't let them cheat the system, the two other officials and the satraps proposed the no-prayer law because they wanted Daniel gone. This is similar to how the Chaldeans "*maliciously accused the Jews*" back in Daniel 3:8. Different empires, same tricks. But none of them were more powerful than God.

- Read the words of Jesus in John 15:18-20. In what ways do the empires of the world today want God's people gone? We see in the New Testament how the Romans treated Jesus, yet the gospel message couldn't be stopped. How does this knowledge help you when you hear about world events today?

Daniel's accusers didn't have it easy. Daniel 6:4 says, "*They could find no ground for complaint or any fault, because he was faithful, and no error or fault was found in him.*" Of course, Daniel was not sinless — but his story points us to the One who is.

- What words describe Jesus in 1 Peter 2:22-23?

- We ourselves can try to be perfectly faithful and faultless, but let's read on to 1 Peter 2:24: What is the only way we can actually "*live to righteousness*"?

The conspirators against Daniel used a tactical plan. The new Medo-Persian Empire had religious factions splitting it apart and causing turmoil. Their plan would help unite the kingdom, focusing on Darius as the peoples' only go-between to their gods for 30 days. "*All*" the government officials agreed (Daniel 6:7). When Darius signed the injunction, it could not be revoked.

- Yet Isaiah 14:27 says, "*For the LORD of hosts has purposed, and who will annul it?*" No one can trick God. Where do you need this reminder today?

DAY 15

DANIEL 6:10-18
Daniel defied the king's decree and was thrown into the den of lions.

Perhaps there have been times in your life when you have felt like everything was stacked against you. Daniel had every reason to feel that way in today's reading: His fellow government officials wanted him gone. They successfully convinced King Darius to sign a decree saying no one could petition gods or men (in other words, no one could pray) for a 30-day period unless they did so through Darius.

- These officials knew something about Daniel: He had a certain habit. What does Daniel 6:10b specifically say Daniel *"had done previously"*?

Daniel was being set up. Yet he did not back down. Like Peter and the apostles said in Acts 5:29, *"We must obey God rather than men."* That's not to say God's people endorse a regular habit of civil disobedience; in fact, Paul said elsewhere, *"Let every person be subject to the governing authorities. For there is no authority except from God, and those that exist have been instituted by God"* (Romans 13:1). But when it comes to choosing between obeying God's clear commands or submitting to a human authority's clear call for disobedience, we obey God.

Daniel had been living by this truth for almost 80 years. As a young teenager, he had refused the king's food (Daniel 1:8) and resolved to live differently because of his faith in God. A lifetime of doing just that had prepared him for this moment in Daniel 6. As biblical scholar Daniel Akin points out, "Christian character is not *forged* in the moment of adversity. Christian character is *revealed* in the moment of adversity."[1]

- What spiritual disciplines do you practice (like prayer, fasting, scripture memorization, meditating on God's Word, etc.) that can prepare you to remain faithful to God whatever the future may hold?

The officials had set their trap for both Daniel and Darius, and it appeared to work. Daniel prayed anyway, just like they thought he would. And Darius couldn't change his injunction, as they were quick to remind him (v. 12). Bible scholar John H. Walton writes that the "royal code of honor would have made it out of the question for the king to rescind an order."[2]

Scripture spends a lot of time focusing on Darius during this event. We learn that Darius was "*much distressed*" (v. 14). He couldn't sleep, couldn't eat (v. 18). And wildly enough, he provided Daniel with truth and encouragement: "*May your God, whom you serve continually, deliver you!*" (v. 16). Darius was a pagan king, yet in his distress, he didn't call on his own gods. He directed Daniel to look to the Lord for his salvation. Some scholars suggest Darius was being sincere. Others say he was being sarcastic. Either way, he spoke the truth!

- God's sovereignty is so great He can even use the mouths of unbelievers to deliver truth and encouragement to His people! What are some ways you have received encouragement from a "worldly" source, and how did this prompt you to turn to God?

Daniel had not done anything to harm the king. The king knew it. Yet when the accusers came, the king felt his hands were tied. So Daniel was thrown in the den of lions, a stone was rolled over the opening, and it was sealed with the king's seal so no one could try to interfere. This passage makes it clear that even the most powerful world ruler is powerless in certain situations. There is only one power we can find confidence in, only one that can keep us safe for eternity: God's power.

In this sense, Daniel's story was a preview for the bigger story that was coming ...

- Fill in the "Jesus" column of the chart below with the similarities you find between Daniel and Jesus.

DANIEL	JESUS
Daniel was framed by accusers.	*Matthew 27:1-2*
Daniel was innocent of crime, except for that of following God at all costs.	*Matthew 27:23*
Darius felt his hands were tied, and he couldn't save Daniel.	*Matthew 27:24*
Daniel was thrown to the lions to die.	*Matthew 27:31*
A stone was rolled over the entrance to the lions' den.	*Matthew 27:60*
The stone was sealed by the government to deter interference.	*Matthew 27:64-66*

- Based on these similarities between Daniel's story and Jesus', how do you predict Daniel's story will end? What assurance does this give you about how *your* story will end if you are in Christ?

ENCOURAGEMENT *through* PRAYING GOD'S WORD

In Daniel 6:10, Daniel went to his room and prayed. While we have no idea what exactly Daniel said, perhaps some words of Scripture came to him at that moment. When we need a source of encouragement, we can always go to God's Word. It has just the words we need.

Psalm 57 is one example of a Bible passage Daniel could have prayed, and we can pray it too. This psalm was written by David when he was fleeing from an angry king (Saul) who wanted him dead — but God had other plans.

PSALM 57

To the choirmaster: according to Do Not Destroy. A Miktam of David, when he fled from Saul, in the cave.

*Be merciful to me, O God, be merciful to me,
for in you my soul takes refuge;
in the shadow of your wings I will take refuge,
till the storms of destruction pass by.
I cry out to God Most High,
to God who fulfills his purpose for me.
He will send from heaven and save me;
he will put to shame him who tramples on me.
Selah
God will send out his steadfast love and his faithfulness!*

*My soul is in the midst of lions;
I lie down amid fiery beasts—
the children of man, whose teeth are spears and arrows,
whose tongues are sharp swords.*

*Be exalted, O God, above the heavens!
Let your glory be over all the earth!*

*They set a net for my steps;
my soul was bowed down.
They dug a pit in my way,
but they have fallen into it themselves. Selah
My heart is steadfast, O God,
my heart is steadfast!
I will sing and make melody!
Awake, my glory!
Awake, O harp and lyre!
I will awake the dawn!
I will give thanks to you, O Lord, among the peoples;
I will sing praises to you among the nations.
For your steadfast love is great to the heavens,
your faithfulness to the clouds.*

*Be exalted, O God, above the heavens!
Let your glory be over all the earth!*

WEEKEND REFLECTION *and* PRAYER

Let's take a look at where we saw God's power at work in this week's study:

First, God's power humbled and then restored a proud King Nebuchadnezzar (Daniel 4).

God's power got the attention of a prideful King Belshazzar with a hand writing mysteries on the palace walls (Daniel 5).

And just as He had foretold, God brought down the Babylonian Empire in one swift night through the Medo-Persian attack (Daniel 5:30-31).

Still, since they didn't follow God, this new empire and new king would have the same problems (Daniel 6:1-4) — because God alone has the power to change hearts.

So the all-sovereign Almighty used the mouth of a pagan king to deliver words of truth: Only God has the power to save (Daniel 6:16).

God can both humble and restore us, and both are for our good. He knows how to get our attention when we get distracted. He reminds us that in this world, people and powers and problems will come and go, but He alone remains unchanged. He alone remains all-powerful. And no matter what is coming up ahead, He alone has the power to save. He always has. He always will.

> *Father God, give me confidence in Your power at work. You are working in my life right now. Even when I don't understand, I will trust You. Even when I get confused and distracted, I know You never leave me. You are strong enough to handle everything that comes my way. You save me in big and little ways every day. I place my faith in You alone. In Jesus' name, amen.*

NOTES

NOTES

WEEK FOUR

DAY 16

DANIEL 6:19-28
God shut the lions' mouths and saved Daniel.

We left off last week in Daniel 6 with Daniel being thrown into the den of lions, the entrance being sealed shut, and King Darius having a rough night. In Daniel 6:19-20, the king anxiously went to the den "*at break of day*" and made a bold declaration: "*O Daniel, servant of the **living God** ...*" (emphasis added).

The king would make a similar statement later, this time to all the peoples, nations and languages of his kingdom, saying, "*for he is the **living God,** enduring forever; his kingdom shall never be destroyed, and his dominion shall be to the end*" (v. 26, emphasis added).

- The same God who was living in Daniel's time is living today and will continue to live forever. What does it mean to you that you serve a living God? What confidence do you find in that truth?

Daniel told the king that God had sent an angel to shut the lions' mouths and that he was not only alive but unharmed (v. 22). Daniel's deliverance came from God alone. Yes, Daniel called himself "*blameless*" before God in verse 22 (which is not to say that he was without sin altogether but that he remained faithful throughout this circumstance). And yes, Daniel had "*trusted in his God*" (v. 23), an obedient and good response to his situation. But it's also clear that Daniel didn't save himself — rather, salvation came from the One he directed his obedience and faith toward.

In the same way, we, too, are to live our lives by faith: Blamelessness and obedience are our responses to the goodness of the gospel in Christ because it is only through Him that we are saved (Romans 1:16-17).

- Looking back over Daniel 6, what or who was Daniel saved from? What have you been saved from through Christ alone?

Daniel 6:24 ends on a dark note. Daniel was rescued, but his accusers were not. This violent ending is a sobering reminder that there is an opposite to salvation. First Thessalonians 1:10 reminds us to look to "*Jesus who delivers us from the wrath to come.*" A time will come when Jesus will return and eternally punish the sins of those who don't follow Him. Because of our sin, all people deserve punishment, but if we trust in Him for salvation, Christ rescues and saves us because He took on the death we deserve.

- It is humbling and important to remember that Jesus took our place in the "lion's den" of punishment for our sin. Write a prayer thanking Jesus that He did this to rescue you forever.

Finally, it is noteworthy that Daniel 6 makes it clear there was no earthly reason why Daniel was spared. The lions had not been tamed, and they were hungry — so hungry that the other people who were thrown into their den were devoured "*before they reached the bottom*" (v. 24). Daniel's escape could only be explained by God's power.

- Sometimes when we experience God's hand at work, our brains try to rationalize the situation by explaining it away in earthly terms or by calling it a coincidence. Why do you think we do this? How can you guard against this in the future?

Like Nebuchadnezzar, King Darius ended up praising "*the God of Daniel*" (v. 26). He decreed these powerful words: "*He delivers and rescues; he works signs and wonders in heaven and on earth, he who has saved Daniel from the power of the lions*" (v. 27).

- To end, let's put everything from today together. Repeat out loud the words of Daniel 6:27. Then end by filling in these blanks to make it personal to yourself: **God has saved _____ from _____.**

DAY 17

DANIEL 7:1-8
Daniel had a vision of four beasts.

What amazing stories we have studied of fiery furnaces, humbled kings and lions' dens! It has been incredible to see how God worked in the lives of these real people. Today's reading brings us to the halfway point in the book of Daniel. Daniel 1-6 included historical narratives, or stories of what happened in the past. Daniel 7 starts the second half of the book, which is what we call apocalyptic literature.

When we hear the term "apocalyptic literature," we may automatically think "end times." But apocalypse in its truest form simply means a revelation (something revealed). With this in mind, we'll learn all about Daniel's visions and what they represent or reveal. Before we dive in, take a moment to read "**Apocalyptic Literature**" on Page 80.

- What are your initial feelings when you hear about apocalyptic literature? Excitement? Nervousness? Confusion? Let's take a moment to ask God for wisdom, peace and understanding. Thank Him that He desires to reveal Truth to you.

The first vision Daniel wrote about came to him during the reign of Belshazzar of Babylon (Daniel 7:1); therefore, we are going back in time to when the Babylonian Empire was on top. In this first vision, Daniel saw four winds stirring up the great sea. This is an image that refers all the way back to the beginning of time, when *"the earth was without form and void, and darkness was over the face of the deep. And the Spirit of God was hovering over the face of the waters"* (Genesis 1:2). The waters represent the chaos and darkness of the world.

From this chaos emerged four beasts (Daniel 7:3-8).

- As you read the descriptions of the four beasts Daniel envisioned, what words come to mind? (Tame or frightening? Docile or fierce? Does the scene appear to be getting more chaotic or less?)

The beasts of Daniel 7 get increasingly *"terrifying and dreadful and exceedingly strong"* (v. 7). This reminds us that our world, because it is fallen (Genesis 3), is headed for increasing chaos and destruction, not order. While this is sobering, it is also a relief to look at our world today and know that none of this is a shock to God. He is not wringing His hands, saying, "Oh no! I didn't see that coming." God knows what is going on. He saw it from the beginning. And He has a plan.

- What global or local event do you need to remember is in the hands and plans of God? How can you pray for that situation this week?

History is full of people who have acted in monstrous ways. They were there in the Babylonian, Medo-Persian, Greek and Roman Empires. We have seen them rise and fall around the world in wars, genocides and more. The emerging horn of the fourth beast in Daniel 7:8 reminds us the future will have monsters as well.

- There are many scriptures that talk about the Antichrist, an end-times opponent and oppressor of God's people, as we will see in the coming days. Today, simply read Revelation 13:1-6. Notice the similarities to Daniel 7's symbolism. What are your thoughts or feelings toward these images, both in Daniel 7 and Revelation 13?

If we stopped our study here, the future would look bleak. Thankfully, tomorrow's verses are filled with hope.

- End today by reading the words of Lamentations 3:21-24. These words were written by a poet who was also in bleak circumstances. Yet what do they remind us about God?

APOCALYPTIC LITERATURE

In the Bible, apocalyptic literature expresses a revelation God gave to someone so as to provide a heavenly perspective on an earthly situation. It is a reminder that more is going on in our world than what meets the eye. And when we see that perspective, it can give us hope and sometimes challenge us to change in light of eternity.

Apocalyptic literature is packed with symbolism. Sometimes its symbols are difficult to understand — in fact, sometimes we won't be able to understand all the details with complete clarity. The prophets themselves often didn't fully understand what God revealed to them (Daniel 7:15-16)! But by using the entire Bible as a guide, we can often see patterns more clearly and gain understanding.[1]

It is also important to remember that biblical prophecy is multilayered. This means it can have one meaning related to the present or near future as well as other layers of meaning for the more distant future. Another term for this is "dual fulfillment." For example, we can see dual fulfillment in Isaiah 7:14, which talks about a son being born and named Immanuel. On the one hand, Isaiah 7:3 mentions that this was to be a sign to King Ahaz, giving scholars reason to believe the prophecy was fulfilled during his reign. On the other hand, Isaiah 7:14 can also be linked with Isaiah 9:6, which spoke of a messianic child who would be called *"Wonderful Counselor, Mighty God, Everlasting Father, Prince of Peace,"* pointing to Jesus, the Son of God, born among us as our Immanuel (Matthew 1:21-23).

We will be keeping all of these nuances of prophecy in mind as we study the second half of Daniel. These visions have so much to teach us about the power of God at work in the world.

WHAT did the BEASTS of DANIEL 7 REPRESENT?

BEAST NO. 1: LION WITH EAGLES' WINGS, MADE TO STAND ON TWO FEET LIKE A MAN.

In Daniel's visions, lion imagery often represents Babylon or Nebuchadnezzar. Lions are a symbol of majestic power. Eagles also show speed and power. Some scholars therefore believe that the wings being *"plucked off"* this beast symbolized the humbling of Nebuchadnezzar and that the phrase *"the mind of a man was given to it"* (Daniel 7:4) referred to his restoration (Daniel 4).

BEAST NO. 2: BEAR RAISED UP ON ONE SIDE.

This beast is often thought to represent the Medo-Persian Empire. Some think the bear was on one side to show the unequal power between the Medes and Persians. The mouth biting three ribs (Daniel 7:5) perhaps symbolizes the three peoples, or three countries, Cyrus conquered in creating the empire: the Medes in northern Iran, the kingdom of Lydia in Anatolia, and the Babylonian Empire.

BEAST NO. 3: LEOPARD WITH FOUR HEADS AND FOUR WINGS OF A BIRD.

Leopards are known for speed and pouncing on their prey. Again, wings signify speed and strength. Many scholars liken this beast to the Greek Empire, noting that Alexander the Great rapidly conquered what was then the known world within 10 short years. The four heads (Daniel 7:6) may represent how the Greek Empire was divided among Alexander's four generals after his death. We will cover this again regarding another vision of Daniel, but these generals oversaw the Ptolemaic (toe·luh·may·ick) kingdom of Egypt, the Seleucid (suh·loo·suhd) Empire in the east, Pergamon in Asia Minor, and Macedon.

BEAST NO. 4: UNLIKE ANY EARTHLY ANIMAL — IRON TEETH, 10 HORNS, WITH A TERRIFYING SMALL HORN EMERGING.

Horns are a symbol of strength; therefore, 10 horns means multiplied strength (Daniel 7:7). Many scholars suggest this fourth beast represented the Roman Empire. In terms of size, strength and longevity, the Roman Empire was unlike anything the world had seen up to that point. Some scholars see this last beast as also representing a future, universal empire where human evil will reach its apex. The small emerging horn (Daniel 7:8) may be a reference to the evil emperor Antiochus IV Epiphanes, but many also understand it to be a reference to the Antichrist.[1]

DAY 18

DANIEL 7:9-14
Daniel saw the Ancient of Days and one like a Son of Man.

Sometimes in important documents, a reader will take a sticker or a highlighter and use it to mark the most important line. Within the Bible, we find a literary device called "chiasm" that serves a similar purpose. Named after the Greek letter *chi*, which is shaped like an X, chiastic structure has a focal point at its center. The basic idea is that words, lines of poetry or events in a story follow a pattern of mirrored repetition (similar to A-B-C-D-C-B-A), and the middle of the pattern contains the most important point.

Many believe the book of Daniel was written with a chiastic structure, making Daniel 7 the most important chapter and the middle of Daniel 7 the most important point. This would be today's reading!

We left Daniel 7:8 with the scary beasts and the creepy little horn with eyes and a mouth. Suddenly, the vision switches gears in today's reading, and we have three different "*I looked*" or "*I saw*" sections.

First, in verses 9-10, Daniel saw the Ancient of Days take His seat on a throne. This is the only Old Testament reference to the "*Ancient of Days.*" Let's break down the images and their symbolism in Daniel 7:9-10.

IMAGE	MEANING
The Ancient of Days	Eternal One who was present before the beginning of time
Clothing white as snow	Purity and goodness: One who can do no wrong
Hair like pure wool	White hair: great wisdom
Flaming throne with burning wheels, fire coming out before Him	Divine presence, power and judgment
Thousand thousands serving Him, 10,000 x 10,000 standing before Him	Innumerable servants: interpreted in light of Revelation 5:11, these are angels worshipping God

- Based on these symbols, we know the Ancient of Days is God. How does this paint a picture of God's character?

Next we reach the second "*I looked*" section in Daniel 7:11-12.

- Remember the fourth beast we talked about yesterday and the little horn that emerged? Daniel called it "*terrifying and dreadful and exceedingly strong*" (v. 7). But how strong was this beast and horn in the presence of God? Who holds all the power in verses 11-12?

The fourth beast is destroyed in one verse! It is easily snuffed out and tossed aside, dwarfed by the Ancient of Days and the One we meet in the final "*I saw*" section (vv. 13-14) — the "*one like a son of man.*"

There are many times in the Old Testament where "son of man" simply refers to a human being. However, this section of Daniel 7 is unique. For one thing, verse 13 says "*like a son of man*" (emphasis added). So the form was human, but it was different from other humans. We also see this Son of Man coming from "*the clouds of heaven*" (v. 13). This immediately implies He is divine. Verse 14 also says "*all peoples ... should serve him.*" And He is "*given ... glory,*" but God doesn't give His glory to anyone besides Himself: "*I am the Lord; that is my name; my glory I give to no other ...*" (Isaiah 42:8). The Son of Man is both human and God.

- We know the Son of Man to be Jesus. He used this title Himself and claimed to fulfill the role in Matthew 24:30 and Matthew 26:64. What similarities do you see between these verses and Daniel 7:13-14?

- The Apostle John also later witnessed an apocalyptic vision similar to Daniel's. What similarities do you find in Revelation 14:14 (written by John) and Daniel 7:13-14?

When Jesus claimed the title Son of Man, the people had to decide if they believed Him to be the coming Messiah whom Daniel had promised. And while Jesus' Kingdom did not look like the earthly kingdom the Jews longed for God to create to save the nation of Israel, it was an even better Kingdom — one for "*all peoples, nations, and languages*" (Daniel 7:14).

- Who holds all the power (dominion, glory and kingdom) in Daniel 7:13-14? For how long?

Seven times so far in our study, we have considered God's power working through Daniel and His "*spirit*" (Daniel 4:8-9; Daniel 4:18; Daniel 5:11-12; Daniel 5:14; Daniel 6:3) — the Holy Spirit of God. Now, Daniel also witnessed a vision of the Father and the Son. We serve one amazing God who exists in three Persons — and Daniel saw just what this all-powerful, triune God can do.

- What confidence can you have in God's power after studying today's reading? How long has God been in power, and how long will He be powerful? What does He have power over specifically in these verses?

DANIEL 7:15-28
Daniel's vision of beasts was interpreted for him.

DAY 19

Often our emotions can feel like a roller coaster ride: up, down and all around. Sometimes we know where they are headed, but sometimes they catch us by surprise. Perhaps Daniel could relate. His vision started with four terrifying beasts, then he unexpectedly saw the Ancient of Days destroying the awful fourth beast, and finally he saw the One like a Son of Man coming from the clouds. What a relief! It looked like everything was going to be OK.

So Daniel should have been OK, too, right? Instead, the text says Daniel was "*anxious*" and "*alarmed*" (Daniel 7:15).

- When have you walked through a scary moment and received reassuring news but eventually went back to worry and fear? Why do you think we do this?

In a sense, it is nice to know we are not the only ones. Daniel struggled with anxiety and pesky alarming thoughts as well. Verse 16 tells us Daniel "*approached one of those who stood there*" in his vision "*and asked him the truth concerning all this.*" When Daniel was worried or confused, he sought help. We, too, can go to trusted friends and especially to God, through prayer and the study of His Word, to find answers and wisdom to strengthen us.

Daniel was told two clear points about his vision:

1. The beasts represented earthly kings/kingdoms (v. 17).
2. The saints of the Most High shall receive the Kingdom that will not pass away (v. 18).

This second point is especially interesting because we saw in verse 14 that the everlasting Kingdom belongs to the One like a Son of Man (that is, Jesus). Yet this is the beauty of the gospel: If we trust in Him, Jesus shares with us everything He acquired in His victory over sin and death! Romans 5:18 says Jesus' "*one act of righteousness leads to justification and life for all*" believers.

- What does it mean to you that Jesus shares with you His victory (Romans 8:37)? What does it mean that followers of the Most High will receive and possess His Kingdom?

Daniel wasn't anxious and alarmed about the everlasting Kingdom. What he was really worried about was this fourth beast with iron teeth, metal legs and frightening horns (Daniel 7:19). And the answer to what this beast represented was not super clear.

Scholars through the ages have had different thoughts. Did the beast and its defeat represent the rise and fall of the Roman Empire, as theologian John Calvin suggested? Was the little horn a reflection of a time period in the Church where there was an abuse of power, as some early Protestant Christians believed? Did it symbolize Antiochus Epiphanes (175-164 B.C.), Nero (A.D. 54-68) or Adolph Hitler (1933-1945)?[1] All of these interpretations may have some validity. We can also look to the future for possible fulfillments: The New Testament repeatedly speaks about a *"man of lawlessness"* (2 Thessalonians 2:3-4), *"abomination of desolation"* (Matthew 24:15), *"antichrist"* (1 John 2:18) or *"beast"* (Revelation 13:1-10) who will appear toward the end of this world.

- Specifically, read 1 John 2:18. What do you learn? In what ways are all evil human attempts for power anti-Christlike?

Daniel 7:25 says this fourth beast/kingdom will rule, persecuting God's people, for *"a time, times, and half a time."* The exact number or length of these "times" is less important than the fact that there is **a specific amount of time** evil will be alloted, and then it will have no more power.

- How does it give you confidence to know that evil has a timeline and will most definitely come to an end?

Lest we get caught up in fear again, the vision interpretation ends with the reminder that though hard things will happen, evil *will* be destroyed, and a great and everlasting Kingdom *is coming* (vv. 26-27). In one sense, because of Jesus, God's Kingdom is already here! He came to tell the world, *"The kingdom of God is at hand; repent and believe in the gospel"* (Mark 1:15).

- Take a moment to bring any fears or anxious thoughts you have about the future to the Ancient of Days. Praise Jesus for giving you His victory over sin and death and for promising you His forever Kingdom.

DAY 20

DANIEL 8:1-14
Daniel had a vision of a ram being overthrown by a goat that grew an evil horn.

Our dreams are typically nothing more than mental imagery our brains create while we sleep. Sometimes they are funny, sometimes just strange, and sometimes really frightening. Yet imagine what Daniel must have felt, knowing the images in his visions were messages from God! We've already studied how in the first year of Belshazzar's reign (Daniel 7:1), Daniel had a vision of four beasts. Then Daniel 7 ended with the prophet feeling alarmed, but he *"kept the matter in [his] heart"* (v. 28).

Two years later, in the third year of Belshazzar's rule, Daniel had another vision (Daniel 8:1). This vision, of a ram and a goat, was no walk in the park either.

Let's take note of the words used to describe the ram in Daniel 8:4b: *"No beast could stand before him, and there was no one who could rescue from his power."* The ram was unstoppable — until he wasn't. When the goat came charging, verse 7 says *"the ram had no power to stand before him ... there was no one who could rescue the ram."*

The ram went from unstoppable to helpless in the blink of an eye. What a reminder of how fickle the rise and fall of power, influence, fame, fortune and any other earthly desire can be. Apart from God, no one and nothing is unstoppable forever.

- Where do you see the quick rising and falling of earthly powers today? What is something you fear that seems unstoppable, and how do today's scriptures remind you that God is the only unstoppable One?

We saw the chaos of earthly kingdoms in Nebuchadnezzar's dream in Daniel 2. We saw it in Daniel's vision of the beasts in Chapter 7. We see it again in Daniel 8. We know through the study of history that chaos and fighting has always been present — and it will continue in the future as well.

- What did Jesus Himself say about war and trouble in Mark 13:7-8?

- It's one thing to be ambushed by trouble. It's another to be told it's coming, even if you don't exactly know how, when or where. How do these verses about future chaos prepare you to walk into the future? How did Jesus reassure His disciples in Mark 13:11 and Mark 13:13?

Once again in Daniel 8, we see an evil little horn. This horn would bring terrible persecution of God's people. Daniel 8:11 goes on to mention that the horn would become "*even as great as the Prince of the host.*" In Hebrew, this is not a name for God used elsewhere in Scripture, but it could be a reference to God, or it could mean a high priest serving in the temple of God. Either way, the horn is trying to **become God**. In doing so, it attempts to trample everything pointing back to God.

- While Isaiah 14:12-16 refers to earthly kings on one level, many scholars believe it also describes the fall of Satan. Jesus also said He "*saw Satan fall like lightning from heaven*" (Luke 10:18). What similarities do you see between Isaiah 14:12-16 and Daniel 8:11-12? What is the fate of those who attempt to overthrow God?

Persecution and pain are hard to think about. In Daniel 8:13, one angel asked a question many of us probably have as well: "*How long*"? How long will suffering last? How long will God's people have to endure?

Here, another angel gave an answer. Scholars are divided about whether "*2,300 evenings and mornings*" in verse 14 means about 3 ½ years (1,150 evenings and 1,150 mornings) or about 7 years (2,300 evenings and 2,300 mornings) or if it refers to God's own unique timetable (2 Peter 3:8). What we do know is that God sovereignly orchestrates time itself. Just as our days are marked out by Him (Job 14:5; Psalm 139:16), so are all the world's days to come.

- Read 1 Peter 5:10. Suffering will only last a little while. Write the four things God will do for you at just the right time, according to this verse:

the RAM and GOAT of DANIEL 8

Still scratching your head over that ram and goat? You're not alone! Our human understanding of God's revelation is limited and imperfect, yet even these limitations remind us that we serve an all-knowing God. We humbly rely on Him to give us the understanding we need.

With that in mind, many interpretations of Daniel 8 focus on how it predicted historical events. See the below examples:

WHAT IS THE RAM WITH TWO HORNS, ONE HORN HIGHER THAN THE OTHER (DANIEL 8:3-4)?

Many scholars agree this represented the Medo-Persian Empire. Horns were a symbol of power and strength. One horn being higher showcased the stronger Persian section of the empire. The ram charged in all directions, just as the Medo-Persians conquered all the surrounding land, eventually becoming simply Persia.

WHAT IS THE GOAT WITH ONE HORN, WHICH BROKE INTO FOUR HORNS (DANIEL 8:5-8)?

This represented the Greek Empire. The Greek army, under the direction of Alexander the Great (the one big horn), swiftly conquered the Persians (note that the goat didn't touch the ground in verse 5, meaning it was very fast). The horn breaking signified Alexander's death. Again, as in Daniel's vision of the leopard with four heads (Daniel 7:6), the four horns demonstrate how the Greek Empire was then split up into four parts. These horns likely represented these four generals: Cassander (in control of Macedonia and Thrace), Lysimachus (Asia Minor), Seleucus (Syria and Mesopotamia), and Ptolemy (Egypt).

WHAT IS THE SMALL, EVIL HORN THAT GROWS OFF THE GOAT (DANIEL 8:9-14)?

During the Greek Empire, around 175 B.C., Antiochus IV came into power. Historical records tell us Antiochus raided Jerusalem multiple times, taking hordes of treasures from the temple and massacring or selling into slavery massive numbers of Jewish people. He also desecrated the temple of God by raising up a statue of Zeus, sacrificing pigs on the altar, and burning Torah (Scripture) scrolls. But just as Daniel 8:14b says *"the sanctuary shall be restored to its rightful state,"* Christ came to rebuild God's temple in an eternal way through His sacrificial death and resurrection (Matthew 26:61; Mark 8:31).

WEEKEND REFLECTION *and* PRAYER

Let's take a look at where we saw God's power at work in this week's study:

First, the power of God shut the mouths of lions and shut the mouths of spiteful people too (Daniel 6).

Then Daniel saw a vision of four beasts that looked especially powerful (Daniel 7:1-8) ...

But these beasts were nothing compared to the power and might of the Ancient of Days and the Son of Man (Daniel 7:9-14). Like the fourth beast with the evil horn in Chapter 7 or the goat with the evil horn in Chapter 8, all evil is on a timeline with an endpoint determined by God. Its days are numbered.

And until the end comes, God proves over and over that He will provide what His people need to endure through the hard moments.

We can place everything into God's hands — because He is the One who holds it all anyway. Our safety, our reputation, our hurts and pains and number of days ... God holds it all. And He promises us that He is in control, even if it all looks like chaos in the world. He has the end set. Sin, death and evil will meet their doom. In the meantime, His power is at work in us, helping us to endure hard times, hold on to hope, and find our strength in Him.

Father God, give me confidence in Your power at work. My entire life is in Your hands. You know what every day of my future holds. You know there will be days of chaos and pain, but You have also promised You will be with me the entire time. You will strengthen me and uphold me. You will help me endure. Thank You that all evil is coming to its end soon. I praise You, Lord. In Jesus' name, amen.

NOTES

NOTES

WEEK FIVE

DANIEL 8:15-27
Daniel's vision of a ram and a goat was interpreted for him.

DAY 21

In Daniel 8, Daniel had a vision of a ram and a goat. Verse 15 says he *"sought to understand it."* And in today's reading, things take a unique turn as we, alongside Daniel, actually get a glimpse into the spiritual realm!

An angel named Gabriel came forward. In the Old Testament, angels are named only in the book of Daniel. Here we meet Gabriel; in Chapter 10, we will meet Michael.

- Read Daniel's reaction to meeting Gabriel in verse 17, and notice the type of message Gabriel delivered. Then read about Zechariah's encounter with Gabriel in Luke 1:11-20 and Mary's encounter in Luke 1:26-33. What similarities do you notice, both in people's reactions and in the role Gabriel seems to have in the heavenly realm?

Gabriel stated directly that the ram in Daniel's vision was Media and Persia, and the goat was Greece. (Remember this vision occurred while the Babylonian Empire was still on top!) The horn in the vision is not directly identified, but as we saw in "**The Ram and Goat of Daniel 8**" on Page 90, most scholars agree the horn was a reference to Antiochus IV.

On coins, Antiochus IV printed his image with the word "Epiphanes," an abbreviation for "god manifest." Because he was always fighting wars and in debt to Rome (the next rising power), he needed money, so he took hordes of treasures from the Jerusalem temple. When Jews tried to rise up, Antiochus IV killed tens of thousands of people, selling tens of thousands more into slavery. He then tried to rid the remaining people of every Jewish practice, saying anyone who participated in Sabbath or circumcision would be put to death. If they were found with a Torah scroll (God's Word), they were put to death. They were forced to make sacrifices to heathen gods and inconceivably tortured in an effort to make them renounce their religion.[1]

Week 5 | 95

But eventually the reign of Antiochus IV did end, and the Jewish book of 2 Maccabees records that "he was seized with a pain in his bowels for which there was no relief and with sharp internal tortures … And so it came about that he fell out of his chariot as it was rushing along and the fall was hard as to torture every limb of his body."[2]

- How do the historical records of Antiochus IV and the interpretation of the horn in Daniel 8:23-25 correspond?

Daniel 8:24 prophesied, *"His power shall be great—but not by his own power."* This man was a puppet for the unseen spiritual enemies of God's people.

- What does Ephesians 6:12 teach us about our enemies today? For those familiar with this verse, see if you can recite it from memory, or consider taking this moment to start memorizing the words.

Daniel's visions remind us that the physical world we live in is not all there is. There is a spiritual realm at play as well. Angels are messengers of God and fight spiritual battles, yet evil forces are also at work. But may we never forget that God's power is the greatest in all realms. Daniel 8:25 says when evil rises up *"against the Prince of princes,"* the evildoer *"shall be broken—but by no human hand."* On one level, this could refer to Antiochus IV falling from his chariot, but it ultimately points to God's power to bring justice against the wicked.

- The battle of good and evil is as old as time. We feel it every day of our lives. But how does Daniel 8 remind us God's power is greater than any other? How does that help you walk through today?

Sometimes we wish we could know the future. Daniel saw but a tiny glimpse, and Scripture says he "*was overcome and lay sick for some days*" (v. 27a). To know all the details of what is coming would be an overwhelming burden for us; only the Lord can carry it. There is a lot we, like Daniel, just do not understand. And that is OK, friend. But we can know one thing: In the end, God wins. And until that day comes, we do what Daniel did.

- According to Daniel 8:27, what did he do after he lay sick? In what ways can you continue your day-to-day activities knowing that, in the end, God wins?

DAY 22

DANIEL 9:1-19
Daniel prayed and made confession for himself and his people.

Prayer is not just a part of the Christian life; it is a vital component of our relationship with our heavenly Father. It puts our hearts in the correct position and renews our minds. And who better to teach us about prayer than a man who was known even to his enemies as someone who loved to pray (Daniel 6:4-10)?

Daniel 9, which contains a prayer of Daniel, starts by giving us a time stamp: *"the first year of Darius"* (v. 1). This was approximately 11 years after the vision Daniel had in Daniel 8. By this time, Daniel would have been in his 80s. And of particular importance is the fact that Babylon had fallen and the Medo-Persian Empire now ruled.

It appears that at this time, Daniel had been studying the book of Jeremiah, where he would have read verses like these:

> *"This whole land shall become a ruin and a waste, and these nations shall serve the king of Babylon seventy years"* (Jeremiah 25:11).

> *"For thus says the LORD: When seventy years are completed for Babylon, I will visit you, and I will fulfill to you my promise and bring you back to this place"* (Jeremiah 29:10).

In Daniel 9:2, Daniel was anticipating that the 70 years of Babylonian exile were almost over for Israel.

Scholars today still have different ideas about these 70 years. Some say the exile began in 605 B.C. (when Daniel and others were first taken to Babylon) and ended with the first return of the exiles in 538 B.C. Others say the exile began when Nebuchadnezzar destroyed Jerusalem in 586 B.C. and ended with the rebuilding of the temple in 515 B.C. Still others see a more symbolic meaning of the 70 as a multiplication of seven, a holy number in Scripture, signifying the completeness of God's law and judgment. To all of these theories, Bible scholar Joyce Baldwin says it well when she says not to "be so preoccupied with numbers as to miss the essential truth which those numbers declare."[1]

For today, let's focus on the truth this number in Daniel 9 declares: God's people had sinned, and they deserved the punishment they received in exile. However, God was gracious and kind, limiting the amount of time His people would suffer. He made a way for them to repent and move back into a relationship with Him.

- God has done the same for you: Your sin debt is paid, perfectly and completely, through the blood of Christ! How does it give you confidence to know this? How does it help you endure any pain and suffering you go through today?

Through studying the book of Jeremiah, Daniel was moved to pray. He allowed Scripture to drive his prayer, and we can do the same.

- When was the last time something you read in Scripture moved you to prayer? How can you use Scripture to drive your prayers in the future?

Daniel 9 is a wonderful example for us to study and follow in prayer. Notice that Daniel didn't go straight into making requests of God but rather began with adoration, calling Him "*great and awesome*" and praising how He "*keeps covenant and steadfast love*" (v. 4).

- Beginning our prayers with adoration helps remind us of whom we are praying to. It puts our focus in the right place. Begin a prayer here with words of adoration to God:

Daniel then moved to confession. This man — who had defied the king's food as a teenager, served faithfully, interpreted dreams under the guidance of the Holy Spirit, prayed three times a day, and was willing to lay down his life for God — did not think of himself as better than the rest of Israel. He said "***we** have not listened*" (v. 6), "*to **us**, O Lord, belongs open shame*" (v. 8), "***we** have rebelled*" (v. 9), and "***all Israel** has transgressed*" (v. 11, emphases added). Bible scholar Herman Veldkamp says, "What distinguishes [believers] from the world is not that we are less wicked but that by the grace of God we have learned to see our wickedness for what it is and that we confess our sins."[2] Praise Jesus that because of Him, we have righteous standing before God, and He changes and renews us to become more like Him every day. But we aren't sinless on this side of heaven — and when we sin, we recognize it and repent.

- It is humbling yet important work to sit and recognize our own sinful behavior. Continue your prayer from above by taking time to confess before the Lord:

It was not until the end of his prayer that Daniel asked something of the Lord. His plea for mercy was dripping with humility. Daniel knew sinful people, including himself, didn't deserve anything from God. But he also knew God is good, merciful and full of love, and his desire was to give God glory (vv. 18-19).

- Finish your prayer today by asking God for what you need or desire. Pray that God's answer would bring Him honor and glory forever and ever.

DANIEL 9:20-27
The angel Gabriel answered Daniel's prayer with a vision of 70 weeks.

DAY 23

If you have ever put together a puzzle, you know how sometimes one piece will make no sense … until you get more and more pieces in place and begin to see the big picture. Then you can begin to understand that piece in your hand.

Earlier in Daniel 9, we saw that Daniel had been studying the book of Jeremiah and read about the 70 years God's people would be in exile. Believing that time to be coming to an end, Daniel began to pray and confess for all Israel. It was during this time of prayer that a familiar visitor came to Daniel: The angel Gabriel had another message. In Daniel 9:23a, Gabriel said, *"At the beginning of your pleas for mercy a word went out, and I have come to tell it to you, for you are greatly loved."*

So many times, even if we believe God has the power to do what we ask, our lack of confidence comes from wondering if our prayers really matter to Him.

- Alongside Daniel 9:23, read 1 John 5:14-15, Hebrews 4:15-16 and James 5:16. What do you learn about prayer from these verses?

Gabriel then began to share with Daniel a vision of *"seventy weeks"* (Daniel 9:24). In the ESV Bible footnotes, you will see that *"weeks"* could also be translated as "sevens." The Hebrew calendar was divided into sevenths, as God told them to rest on the seventh day of the week and on every seventh year. Most scholars agree the timelines presented here are therefore to be regarded in terms of years. However, as to when these timelines begin and end, and what they mean, scholars are divided.

- Read "**4 Different Views on the 70 Weeks of Daniel 9:24-27**" on Page 104. Which view do you find particularly interesting? What, if anything, do all of these views have in common?

Week 5 | 101

While there are different opinions on when these 70 "weeks" took and/or will take place, in Daniel 9:24, Gabriel gave a detailed list of what will occur during this time period:

> TRANSGRESSION AND REBELLION WILL BE FINISHED.
> SIN WILL BE PUT TO AN END.
> INIQUITY WILL BE ATONED FOR.
> EVERLASTING RIGHTEOUSNESS WILL BE BROUGHT IN.
> VISION AND PROPHECY WILL BE SEALED UP.
> THE MOST HOLY PLACE (OR HOLY ONE) WILL BE ANOINTED.

- When we read this list as believers in Jesus, the work of Christ hopefully comes to mind! Remember that Daniel was written well before the earthly life of Christ. In what ways does seeing Christ's fulfillment of this prophecy give you confidence in God's power at work?

Gabriel described to Daniel that the first seven "weeks" would consist of restoring and building Jerusalem. The next 62 "weeks" would include building but in a troubled time (v. 25). Toward the end of the 62 "weeks," the anointed one would be "*cut off,*" and the city and temple would be destroyed (v. 26). And in the last "week," there would rise a ruler (similar to the little horn we have seen in past visions) who would lead people to stop worshipping God and usher in "*abominations,*" a word commonly used in Scripture to reference idolatry. All this would continue "*until the decreed end is poured out on the desolator*" (v. 27).

There is a **decreed end** for evil. The end has been put into place and marked by God.

- In 2 Thessalonians 2:8 and Revelation 19:19-21, what other details do you see about how evil will end?

Daniel 9 began with Daniel reading about 70 years. But Gabriel came with a vision of 70 x 7. The picture was so much bigger than the small part Daniel could see in that moment. And the same is true today. While it can be easy for us to focus on what we are going through right here and now, it is also important to remember there is a much bigger story in motion here, and God knows and sees it all perfectly.

- Isaiah 25:1 says, *"O LORD, you are my God; I will exalt you; I will praise your name, for you have done wonderful things, plans formed of old, faithful and sure."* Why might it be important for us today to remember the big picture of God's plans?

4 DIFFERENT VIEWS *on the* 70 WEEKS (70 SEVENS) *of* DANIEL 9:24-27

The following is a sampling of some of the main Christian interpretations of the 70 weeks in Daniel 9. There may be other views, too, but we've limited it to four here for simplicity's sake.

VIEW NO. 1 | MACCABEAN VIEW

This view sees 70 "weeks" (70 sevens, or 490) as a literal timeline, beginning in either 605 B.C. when the first of the Jewish people were exiled or in 586 B.C. when Jerusalem fell to Babylon. The 70th seven then occurred around 164 B.C., the time Judas Maccabeus cleansed the temple and Antiochus IV died (the evil ruler of Greece we learned about in Daniel 8). As with other views we will see, some have pointed out this is not exactly 490 years.

605/586 B.C. — 7 "WEEKS" + 62 "WEEKS" — **164 B.C.**

exile begins — *70th "week": Maccabeus cleanses temple*

VIEW NO. 2 | PRETERIST VIEW

This view sees the 70 weeks as symbolic. The "weeks" or "sevens" in this view began around 538 B.C., when Cyrus issued a decree allowing Jews to return to Jerusalem to rebuild. The first 69 "sevens" then ended around the time of Jesus' baptism, and the 70th "seven" lasted until the destruction of Jerusalem in A.D. 70.

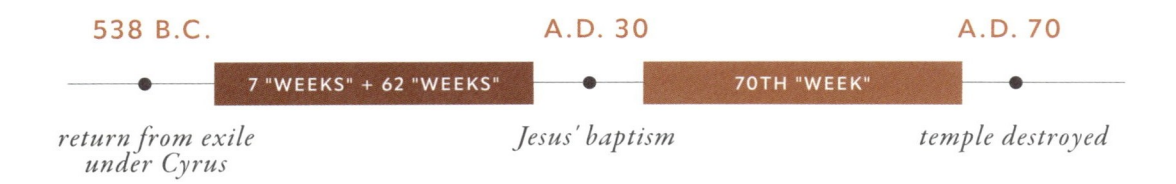

538 B.C. — 7 "WEEKS" + 62 "WEEKS" — **A.D. 30** — 70TH "WEEK" — **A.D. 70**

return from exile under Cyrus — *Jesus' baptism* — *temple destroyed*

VIEW NO. 3 | COVENANTAL VIEW

This view also sees the time periods as symbolic. Like view No. 2, the Covenantal View argues that the "weeks" began in 538 B.C., and the first 69 "sevens" ended when the Messiah was "cut off" and confirmed a new covenant. The difference is that this view sees the 70th "seven" as the present age, lasting until the second coming of Christ. This view sees the destruction of the temple in Jerusalem (A.D. 70) as the "middle" of the 70th "seven."

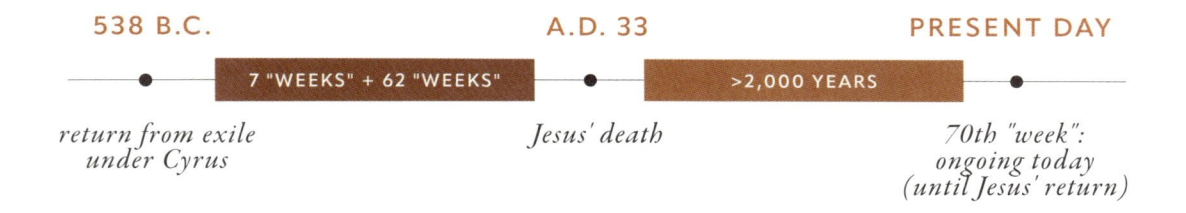

538 B.C. — 7 "WEEKS" + 62 "WEEKS" — **A.D. 33** — >2,000 YEARS — **PRESENT DAY**

return from exile under Cyrus — *Jesus' death* — *70th "week": ongoing today (until Jesus' return)*

VIEW NO. 4 | GAP VIEW OR DISPENSATIONAL VIEW

This view sees the time periods as literal but with a gap (sometimes called "The Great Parenthesis") between the 69th and 70th "weeks." The term "weeks" is seen as a reference to 7 years. This view suggests the "weeks" began around 458 B.C., when Artaxerxes issued a decree allowing Jews to return to Jerusalem. The seven "weeks" (or 49 years) before the *"coming of an anointed one"* plus 62 "weeks" (or 434 years) before the anointed one is *"cut off"* (Daniel 9:26) equals 69 "weeks" (or 483 years). This would bring us to about A.D. 26-27 in the time of Christ. Then we enter the gap, which is the age of the Church. Some dispensationalists believe the 70th "week" will begin at the time of a rapture, with a period of seven years where the Antichrist reigns on earth, until the second coming of Christ.

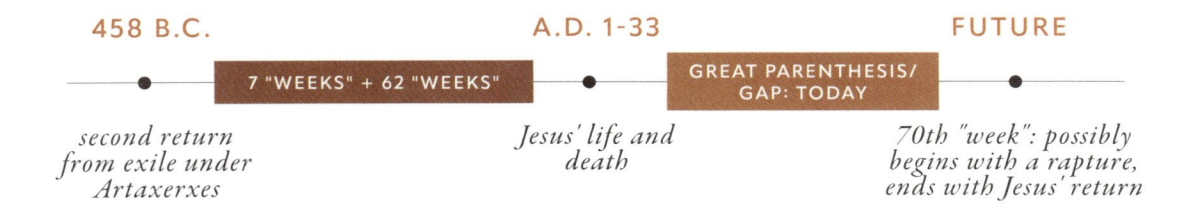

458 B.C. — 7 "WEEKS" + 62 "WEEKS" — **A.D. 1-33** — GREAT PARENTHESIS/GAP: TODAY — **FUTURE**

second return from exile under Artaxerxes — *Jesus' life and death* — *70th "week": possibly begins with a rapture, ends with Jesus' return*

DAY 24

DANIEL 10:1-9
Daniel's final vision began with a man.

Perhaps you have envisioned what it will be like to see Jesus in eternity — the look in His eye, the expression on His face, and the way you will respond. How exciting to know that this will one day be a reality for all believers! Until that glorious day, perhaps we can lean in and listen closely to this final vision that Daniel records. It is by far the longest and most detailed of his visions, revealing conflicts in heaven and earth as well as a final conflict where God ultimately triumphs. Today's reading will focus on the first part of Daniel's vision, where he saw *"a man clothed in linen"* (Daniel 10:5).

Because of Daniel's attention to dating his visions, we can deduce that this vision occurred approximately two years after the vision of Daniel 9. Once again, Daniel would have been an older man, probably in his 80s, at this time. Daniel 10:1 says *"a word was revealed to Daniel,"* and *"the word was true, and it was a great conflict."* It is an ominous beginning to the chapter — appropriately so, as we will see. This *"great conflict"* describes the war Daniel saw coming in the vision, and it also hints at the struggle and pain Daniel would go through to receive the vision.

- Why might it have been a *"great conflict"* (v. 1) or struggle for Daniel to receive this vision? (Look at verses 8-9 for one thought.) How does knowing that Daniel went through suffering to receive this revelation make us more appreciative and respectful of the words we read?

A decree from Cyrus had allowed the first set of Jewish exiles to return to Jerusalem during this time. Reports of the opposition and struggles they faced would have now started trickling back to Persia, where Daniel was. Perhaps this is why Daniel decided to go into *"mourning for three weeks"* (v. 2).

- When was the last time news from family or friends brought you to your knees in grief and prayer? How confident were you that your prayer would result in God's power working in that situation? You can be honest here.

During his time of mourning, Daniel's vision of a man began. There is some scholarly debate about who this man was exactly.

Some believe he was Gabriel. (Critics of this theory wonder why Gabriel would be referred to by name elsewhere in the book of Daniel but not here.)

Others suggest this was a theophany or Christophany, a pre-incarnate appearance of Christ. (Critics of this theory wonder why Christ would say in verse 13 that He needed angels to "*help*" Him. Advocates of this theory counter by saying that the heavenly being of verse 13 is an angelic being, different from the Christ "*man*" in verses 5-9.)

Still others say this man was an angelic being from heaven whose *"face like the appearance of lightning"* reflected the glory and splendor of the God he served (v. 6).

There is merit to all of these theories, but for today, let's study some verses that seem to support the idea of a Christophany.

- Revelation 1:12-17 and Ezekiel 1:26-28 both record visions from God, much like Daniel's. Fill in the chart below with the similarities you find between these visions, placing an X in the columns where similarities are shared. (We've completed the first row for you as an example.)

DANIEL 10:5-6	REVELATION 1:12-17	EZEKIEL 1:26-28
FIGURE LOOKED LIKE A MAN	X	X
CLOTHED IN LINEN		
BELT OF GOLD		
BODY LIKE BERYL *(an aqua/emerald-colored gem)*		
FACE LIKE LIGHTNING		
EYES LIKE TORCHES		
ARMS AND LEGS LIKE BRONZE		
VOICE LIKE THE SOUND OF A MULTITUDE		

Also strikingly similar is the reaction of humans upon seeing the glory of God.

- Read Daniel 10:8-9, Revelation 1:17 and Ezekiel 1:28b. What was each man's reaction?

We have a tendency today to view Jesus as our friend — and He is (John 15:15)! We also call God our Father, and this, too, is right and true. But let us not forget Jesus paid a high price for our sin in order to give us friendship with God (1 Peter 3:18), who is also a Judge and King. It is healthy to be reminded of just how small and frail we are in the presence of the Almighty.

- Bible scholar Ligon Duncan says, "In the Bible, intimacy with God always leaves its mark."[1] What does that statement mean to you? How did it apply to Daniel, and how might it apply to you?

DANIEL 10:10-21
A heavenly messenger strengthened Daniel.

DAY 25

When you feel overwhelmed, where do you go to find a helping hand? Yesterday we looked at different theories as to who exactly Daniel saw in his vision of a man in Daniel 10:5-6, but one thing we know is that the vision caused Daniel to fall down unconscious (v. 9). Today's reading begins with "*a hand*" that reached out to touch Daniel and sit him back up (v. 10).

Some believe this hand belonged to the man (potentially Christ) from Daniel's vision, yet others say this was someone different. Most agree this speaker was a heavenly messenger of some kind sent to strengthen and encourage Daniel. Let's take a look at their interaction.

First, the messenger told Daniel he was "*greatly loved*" (v. 11). He would say it again in verse 19. This is an important statement: Loving someone means listening to them and caring about what they are going through. God feels that way toward us! These verses give us a heavenly perspective on prayer. **Because God loves us,** our prayers are special to Him.

The messenger also told Daniel, "*Your words have been heard.*" More than that, he said they were heard "*from the first day that you set your heart to understand and humbled yourself before your God.*" God hears His people. The messenger then said to Daniel, "*I have come **because of your words***" (v. 12, emphasis added). Daniel's prayer caused movement in the heavenly realm. That truth is mind-blowing! Our prayers can prompt angels and stir movement in the spiritual realm.

- Yesterday we responded honestly about how confident we were that our prayers will result in God's power working in a situation. How does today's reading give you confidence as you pray?

The messenger went on to tell Daniel that he had been delayed by "*the prince of the kingdom of Persia*" or "*kings of Persia*" (v. 13). Scholars say these could be references to demonic powers. The book of Daniel makes it clear there is a war taking place between God's angels and evil spiritual forces who are attempting to control the powers of this world and to inflict havoc on God's people. That is a startling reality. However, the words of John Piper, in his commentary on Daniel 10, ring true: "Be ready for the extraordinary as well as the ordinary ways that evil spirits work. Don't be presumptuous, as though demons were weak; and don't be anxious, as though they were stronger than Jesus."[1]

- How often do you think about activity in the spiritual realm? Why do you think it might be important to remember but not to obsess over?

Next, we are introduced to the second angel with a given name in the book of Daniel: Michael (v. 13). Many scholars believe the archangel Michael has been assigned by God to watch over and protect Israel and the Jewish people.[2]

- Look up these verses that talk specifically about the angel Michael: Daniel 10:13, Daniel 10:21, Daniel 12:1, Jude 1:9 and Revelation 12:7. Write down what you learn about him.

All of this information about angels and demons and spiritual warfare took its toll on Daniel.

- What words describe Daniel's physical reaction in Daniel 10:10-11 and verses 15-17?

Over and over in today's reading, Scripture says a heavenly being touched Daniel, sat him up, spoke encouraging words and strengthened him. The words God had for Daniel completely overwhelmed him, but God didn't leave him in that state. Daniel was stripped of his own strength so that God would be his strength.

- Read the words of the Apostle Paul in 2 Corinthians 12:9-10. They may already be very familiar, so read them slowly and meditate on them. How does this verse go with today's reading, and how does it give you confidence in God's power at work in your life?

WEEKEND REFLECTION *and* PRAYER

Let's take a look at where we saw God's power at work in this week's study:

First, Daniel saw a vision of Persia and Greece, along with a particularly evil ruler, but he was told God would have the ultimate power in this situation (Daniel 8).

Then Daniel read about Israel's 70 years of exile and recognized that they needed God's power. Therefore, he prayed and confessed (Daniel 9:1-19).

Gabriel came as an answer to Daniel's prayer and assured him through the vision of 70 weeks that God knew the future and had powerfully decreed the end of evil (Daniel 9:20-27).

Daniel then had a vision of a man in terrifying radiance and glory, and it was so powerful that it knocked Daniel out completely (Daniel 10:1-9).

And while it is true that the reality of the spiritual world and warfare was overwhelming to Daniel, God did not leave him crushed. In His power, He sent help, encouragement and strength (Daniel 10:10-19).

We, too, can have confidence that God's power is in control of each and every situation we face. When we need to be reminded of this fact, all we have to do is stop and pray. God will remind us that one day, evil will end. He is more powerful than any other force in this world or the spiritual world. Nothing will stand against Him. And while we wait for Him to move and act on our behalf, we can know He promises to strengthen, encourage and help us through it all.

Father God, give us confidence in Your power at work. We praise You, for You are in control. You have decreed an end to evil! You are more powerful than anything in this earthly realm or any other. So we pray, and we confess, and we ask You to strengthen us with Your power today. In Jesus' name, amen.

NOTES

NOTES

WEEK SIX

DANIEL 11:1-19
A vision was given regarding the future kings of the south and north.

DAY 26

Whether you are a history buff or you found yourself falling asleep during world civilizations class in school ... today's lesson will be quite an amazing ride! In Daniel 11, we are going to see God's power displayed through the details of another one of Daniel's visions. To fully appreciate that power, we are going to dive deep into ancient Greek history to see how the prophecies played out.

Before we begin, we want to acknowledge that some Christians may have different interpretations of these verses, but the views we've chosen to present are some of the most widely accepted. As we've discussed, apocalyptic literature often entails multiple layers of symbolism and can have multiple meanings and fulfillments.

As we also mentioned earlier in our study, *"Darius the Mede"* (Daniel 11:1) was probably a title for the Persian King Cyrus. Daniel 11:2 mentions that three more kings would arise in Persia, and the fourth would "*stir up all against the kingdom of Greece.*"

Here are some historical facts about the kings of Persia after Cyrus:

1. Cambyses reigned 530-522 B.C.
2. Smerdis reigned 522 B.C.
3. Darius reigned 522-486 B.C.
4. Xerxes I reigned 486-464 B.C. and invaded Greece, only to be defeated at the Battle of Salamis in 480 B.C.

- How does this history align with Daniel 11:2?

Other, lesser Persian kings reigned as the Persian Empire began to crumble and was eventually brought down by Alexander the Great around 334 B.C. Daniel 11:3-4 describes a mighty king (likely Alexander) who would arise, but "*as soon as he ha[d] arisen,*" his kingdom would be broken and scattered to the four winds, not inherited by those of his own flesh and blood.

Historically, the Greek Empire indeed broke into four parts: south, west, east and north. Ptolemy I was a prominent and successful general under Alexander the Great, and he took control of the Egyptian region to the south. Seleucus I started out as a lesser general, and he took the Babylonian region. However, that region was taken away from him by Antigonus I (another general of Alexander). Seleucus I fled to Egypt and served under Ptolemy I until he gained back his Babylonian territory. Seleucus I then took over not only Babylon but also Syria and Media, increasing his power and territory in a mighty way. This may describe why verse 5 says the south would be strong, but one of his "*princes*" would be stronger.

- It is fascinating to see this history line up with the words of Daniel 11:3-5. Today we have the advantage of being able to see how everything played out exactly as God said it would. How do you think these verses helped God's people when the chaos of their day felt confusing or out of control?

After Alexander, the southern Egyptian region (known as the Ptolemaic Empire) and the northern Babylonian region (known as the Seleucid Empire) became the two powerhouses.

- Read Daniel 11:6-19 carefully. Then complete the activities titled **"Kings of the South (Ptolemaic Empire)"** and **"Kings of the North (Seleucid Empire)"** on Pages 118-123. (Note: Just complete the parts indicated by a green vertical stripe for today's study. The orange ones we'll get to tomorrow.) This may take some time, but allow yourself to be in awe of the wide range of details God provided in this vision and how those details played out perfectly.

Today's passage is mind-blowing — so much so that many secular historians do not accept that Daniel 11 was written before the actual historical events took place. But we know our God has the power to see and direct the future perfectly.

- Today's study of Daniel 11 strengthens our confidence that God is in the smallest details of history and also sees the entire big picture. Write down as many areas as you can think of, both in the world at large and in your personal life, where you need to be reminded that God is currently at work:

- Let's end today by writing a prayer of praise to the God who ordains every detail.

PTOLEMY I SOTER: Prominent and successful general under Alexander the Great. (See Daniel 11:5.)

PTOLEMY II PHILADELPHUS: In an effort to make an alliance with the growing Seleucid Empire, Ptolemy II sent his daughter, Berenice, to marry Antiochus II. She and Antiochus II were poisoned to death by Antiochus II's first wife, Laodice. Ptolemy II died the same year his daughter Berenice was killed. (See Daniel 11:5-6.)

PTOLEMY III EUERGETES: Ptolemy III was the brother of Berenice. In retaliation against her death, he invaded the Seleucid Empire. He returned to Egypt many of the treasures that had been taken from the area in earlier wars. (See Daniel 11:7-8.)

PTOLEMY IV PHILOPATER: Ptolemy IV fought off invasions and attacks from Antiochus III and gained a massive victory at Raphia in Palestine. Under Ptolemy IV's hand, the north suffered massive losses. However, Ptolemy IV's victory would be short-lived, and the Ptolemaic Empire would begin losing power. (See Daniel 11:10-13.)

PTOLEMY V EPIPHANES: Instability surrounded Ptolemy V's reign. Especially noteworthy is that a large number of Jews were unhappy about the heavy taxation and planned a rebellion to overthrow the Egyptian rule. However, they were quickly defeated, and the Jewish leaders were punished. (Interestingly, Ptolemy V married the daughter of Antiochus III the Great in an attempted alliance. This daughter was named Cleopatra I — not to be confused with the famous Cleopatra who married Julius Caesar). (See Daniel 11:14.)

PTOLEMY VI PHILOMETER: Son of Ptolemy V and Cleopatra I, he fought back against the northern king Antiochus IV (who was actually his uncle) but lost and became a hostage. He would make an alliance with Antiochus IV to get his throne back from his brother (Ptolemy VIII), who had taken it while Ptolemy VI was being held hostage. Ptolemy VI intended to use the opportunity for his own gain (as did Antiochus IV). The two would continue to fight against each other. (See Daniel 11:25-27.)

DANIEL 11:5: *"Then the king of the south shall be strong…"*

DANIEL 11:5-6: *"… but one of his princes shall be stronger than he and shall rule, and his authority shall be a great authority. After some years they shall make an alliance, and the daughter of the king of the south shall come to the king of the north to make an agreement. But she shall not retain the strength of her arm, and he and his arm shall not endure, but she shall be given up, and her attendants, he who fathered her, and he who supported her in those times."*

DANIEL 11:7-8: *"And from a branch from her roots one shall arise in his place. He shall come against the army and enter the fortress of the king of the north, and he shall deal with them and shall prevail. He shall also carry off to Egypt their gods with their metal images and their precious vessels of silver and gold, and for some years he shall refrain from attacking the king of the north."*

DANIEL 11:10-13: *"His sons shall wage war and assemble a multitude of great forces, which shall keep coming and overflow and pass through, and again shall carry the war as far as his fortress. Then the king of the south, moved with rage, shall come out and fight against the king of the north. And he shall raise a great multitude, but it shall be given into his hand. And when the multitude is taken away, his heart shall be exalted, and he shall cast down tens of thousands, but he shall not prevail. For the king of the north shall again raise a multitude, greater than the first …"*

DANIEL 11:14: *"In those times many shall rise against the king of the south, and the violent among your own people shall lift themselves up in order to fulfill the vision, but they shall fail."*

DANIEL 11:25-27: *"And he shall stir up his power and his heart against the king of the south with a great army. And the king of the south shall wage war with an exceedingly great and mighty army … And as for the two kings, their hearts shall be bent on doing evil. They shall speak lies at the same table, but to no avail, for the end is yet to be at the time appointed."*

SELEUCUS I NICATOR: Originally a lesser general under Alexander the Great. Fled his Babylonian region and served under Ptolemy I in Egypt for a time before returning to Babylon. Seleucus I then took additional territory and became a strong empire. (See Daniel 11:3-4.)

ANTIOCHUS I SOTER: *(No Direct biblical reference)*

ANTIOCHUS II THEOS: Antiochus II planned to divorce his wife, Laodice, and disinherit her sons, in an agreement he made with Ptolemy II to marry his daughter Berenice and have a child to rule over the Seleucid Empire. However, Laodice had both Antiochus II and Berenice poisoned. (See Daniel 11:6.)

SELEUCUS II CALLINICUS: There are no historical records that Seleucus invaded Egypt. It could be that he thought about it but quickly retreated. (See Daniel 11:9.)

SELEUCUS III CERAUNUS: Son of Seleucus II. Along with his brother, Antiochus III, he continued skirmishes with the Ptolemies. He was murdered after a short reign. (See Daniel 11:10.)

ANTIOCHUS III (THE GREAT): Son of Seleucus II and brother to Seleucus III, he fought against the Ptolemies (the south). After his brother's death, he took control and made the Seleucid Empire into a strong nation with a massive army. He campaigned in Phoenicia and Palestine and went as far as Raphia in southwest Gaza. He used the death of Ptolemy IV to invade Egyptian territory, conquering the well-fortified city of Gaza in 201 B.C. and winning the Battle of Panium in 198 B.C. The Egyptian forces were in retreat, and Egyptian general Scopas finally surrendered. This allowed Antiochus III control of Phoenicia and Palestine (the biblical promised land of the Jews). This event led to Egypt being forced into an alliance with Antiochus III. He sent his daughter to marry Ptolemy V, hoping her offspring could then rule Egypt, but his daughter supported Ptolemy V and not her father. Antiochus III then set his eyes on the coastlands of Greece, but he was ultimately defeated by Rome and forced to sign a treaty at Apanea in 188 B.C. He was also forced to pay a large tribute to Rome. As he returned home, he tried to pillage a temple of Zeus to help pay the heavy tribute but was killed by an angry mob. (See Daniel 11:13, 15-19.)

SELEUCUS IV PHILOPATER: Son of Antiochus III the Great. He sent a "tax collector" to collect money to pay the yearly Roman tribute. He was killed not by an angry mob (like his father) or in battle but by his own tax collector, Heliodorus. His son, Demetrius I Soter, would have been next to take the throne, but he was imprisoned in Rome. (See Daniel 11:20.)

DANIEL 11:3-4: *"Then a mighty king shall arise, who shall rule with great dominion and do as he wills. And as soon as he has arisen, his kingdom shall be broken and divided toward the four winds of heaven ..."*

(No Direct biblical reference)

DANIEL 11:6: *"After some years they shall make an alliance, and the daughter of the king of the south shall come to the king of the north to make an agreement. But she shall not retain the strength of her arm, and he and his arm shall not endure, but she shall be given up, and her attendants, he who fathered her, and he who supported her in those times."*

DANIEL 11:9: *"Then the latter shall come into the realm of the king of the south but shall return to his own land."*

DANIEL 11:10: *"His sons shall wage war and assemble a multitude of great forces, which shall keep coming and overflow and pass through, and again shall carry the war as far as his fortress."*

DANIEL 11:13, 15-19: *"For the king of the north shall again raise a multitude, greater than the first. And after some years he shall come on with a great army and abundant supplies ... Then the king of the north shall come and throw up siegeworks and take a well-fortified city. And the forces of the south shall not stand, or even his best troops, for there shall be no strength to stand. But he who comes against him shall do as he wills, and none shall stand before him. And he shall stand in the glorious land, with destruction in his hand. He shall set his face to come with the strength of his whole kingdom, and he shall bring terms of an agreement and perform them. He shall give him the daughter of women to destroy the kingdom, but it shall not stand or be to his advantage. Afterward he shall turn his face to the coastlands and shall capture many of them, but a commander shall put an end to his insolence. Indeed, he shall turn his insolence back upon him. Then he shall turn his face back toward the fortresses of his own land, but he shall stumble and fall, and shall not be found."*

DANIEL 11:20: *"Then shall arise in his place one who shall send an exactor of tribute for the glory of the kingdom. But within a few days he shall be broken, neither in anger nor in battle."*

ANTIOCHUS IV EPIPHANES:

Also a son of Antiochus III the Great. When his brother Seleucus IV died, Antiochus IV used the opportunity to pay important people to support him as the next king instead of Seleucus IV's son, Demetrius I. (This is the same Antiochus IV we looked at when we studied the "little horn" of Daniel 8.)

Eventually he brought an army against Egypt and defeated Ptolemy VI, taking him hostage. He then made an alliance with Ptolemy VI, allowing him to return to Egypt. It was an alliance neither would keep. Without warning, Antiochus IV invaded Egyptian territory, plundering and dividing the riches among his soldiers.

After plundering Egypt, Antiochus IV returned home by way of Palestine, where he found a Jewish insurrection going on. From that moment forward, he dealt with the Jewish people in ruthless brutality.

Later, he again attempted to invade Egypt but suffered a humiliating defeat, as the Ptolemies had joined forces with the Roman army. (Note: *Kittim* in Daniel 11:30 was a word used to describe the lands around the Mediterranean Sea, where Rome was.) As he retreated out of Egypt, Antiochus IV turned his anger toward Palestine. He decided to reward any Jew who would forsake Judaism to support his Greek ideals, and those who did not, he would torture or kill. He set up an altar and statue devoted to Zeus (Jupiter) in the temple of Jerusalem, then offered sacrifices that were sacrilegious to Jews.

This eventually led to the Maccabean Revolt in 167 B.C., when many faithful Jews organized behind the priest Mattathias and his five sons. They eventually regained Jerusalem, and the temple was reconsecrated, an event now commemorated by Jews in the celebration of Hanukkah.

DANIEL 11:21-35:

Verse 21: *"In his place shall arise a contemptible person to whom royal majesty has not been given. He shall come in without warning and obtain the kingdom by flatteries."*

Verses 22-24: *"Armies shall be utterly swept away before him and broken, even the prince of the covenant. And from the time that an alliance is made with him he shall act deceitfully, and he shall become strong with a small people. Without warning he shall come into the richest parts of the province, and he shall do what neither his fathers nor his fathers' fathers have done, scattering among them plunder, spoil, and goods. He shall devise plans against strongholds, but only for a time."*

Verse 28: *"And he shall return to his land with great wealth, but his heart shall be set against the holy covenant. And he shall work his will and return to his own land."*

Verses 29-32: *"At the time appointed he shall return and come into the south, but it shall not be this time as it was before. For ships of Kittim shall come against him, and he shall be afraid and withdraw, and shall turn back and be enraged and take action against the holy covenant. He shall turn back and pay attention to those who forsake the holy covenant. Forces from him shall appear and profane the temple and fortress, and shall take away the regular burnt offering. And they shall set up the abomination that makes desolate. He shall seduce with flattery those who violate the covenant, but the people who know their God shall stand firm and take action."*

Verses 33-35: *"And the wise among the people shall make many understand, though for some days they shall stumble by sword and flame, by captivity and plunder. When they stumble, they shall receive a little help. And many shall join themselves to them with flattery, and some of the wise shall stumble, so that they may be refined, purified, and made white, until the time of the end, for it still awaits the appointed time."*

Black Sea

Mediterranean Sea

DIVISION *of the* EMPIRE *of* ALEXANDER *the* GREAT

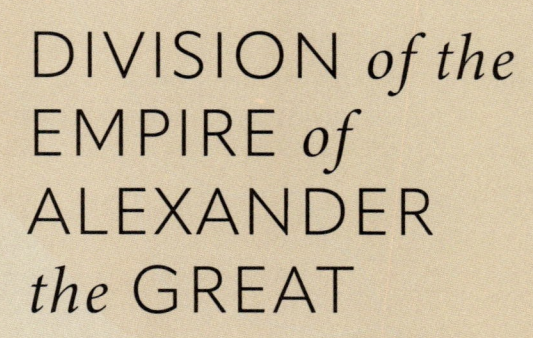

- ■ PTOLEMAIC EMPIRE
- ■ SELEUCID EMPIRE
- ■ MACEDONIA AND THRACE
- ■ LYSIMACHUS EMPIRE

Caspian Sea

Persian Gulf

DAY 27

DANIEL 11:20-35
The kings of the south and north continued in evil for an appointed time.

Yesterday we looked at the first part of the vision of the kings of the south and north in Daniel 11 and how those events lined up with the historical records we have. Absolutely astonishing! Today, we will continue studying this vision and how it aligns with history.

- Flip back to **"Kings of the South (Ptolemaic Empire)"** and **"Kings of the North (Seleucid Empire)"** on Pages 118-123, and based on today's reading, complete the parts of the activity indicated by an orange vertical stripe.

    (A few notes as you study: The *"prince of the covenant"* of verse 22 is most likely Ptolemy VI, as he made a "covenant" with Antiochus IV. Also, Daniel 11:25-27 goes back to the beginning of the conflict between Ptolemy VI and Antiochus IV and so is a retelling of verses 22-23. Finally, when Daniel 11:28 says *"he shall return to his land,"* "he" refers to the king of the north.)

If you weren't able to match up every single detail of these prophecies and timelines, don't worry: Part of the purpose of this exercise is to appreciate how complex these details are — and how God was in charge of *all of them*. With that in mind, let's take a look at some of the lessons we can gather.

Verse 21 speaks of a king of the north (Antiochus IV) who took the throne *"by flatteries."* Later, in verse 32, it says he was able to *"seduce with flattery"* some of God's people into abandoning their customs and beliefs. While the king used unjust laws, deceit, war, force, torture and other evils to get his way, it seems flattery was one of his favorite tactics.

- In what ways is flattery a dangerous tactic of evil? How might you recognize it when you see it, and in what ways can you guard your own heart and mind against such tactics?

We have mentioned before how biblical prophecy is often layered. It can refer to a time in the present or near future and also to events far in the future. The words of Daniel 11:32-35 operate on this principle. On one hand, these events were fulfilled at the time of the Maccabean Revolt, when God's people were persecuted and refined by the fire of trials under Antiochus IV. Yet verses 32-35 also look to the early Church, and *"until the time of the end,"* this prophecy will remain relevant to followers of Jesus.

- Read the words of Jesus in Matthew 24:9-14. What can we expect as we await Jesus' return? What (or who) is our hope when we experience these things?

So much important history has been covered in today's verses. Yet in the midst of all this, there is an idea that keeps repeating and demands to be noted.

- What is *"appointed"* in Daniel 11:27, Daniel 11:29 and Daniel 11:35?

- The word "appointed" means "decided on beforehand." What do we learn from this phrase, and most importantly, who does this appointing?

Week 6 | 127

DAY 28

DANIEL 11:36-45
The vision showed the king of the north growing in terror until the time of the end comes.

Over the past two days, we've looked deeply into the kings of the south and north, and yesterday we focused on how Daniel 11:21-35 closely described Antiochus IV. These verses kept reminding us that Antiochus IV's reign was limited to *"the appointed time."* However, verse 35 also used the phrase *"the time of the end."* This serves as a transition point between the verses we have just studied and today's reading.

Some scholars believe verses 36-45 continue describing the life of Antiochus IV. Others say many of the events in this section do not follow Antiochus IV's life. While he did think of himself as a god, verse 37 says *"he shall not pay attention to any other god"* — yet Antiochus IV was also a devout follower of Zeus. He never again invaded Egypt after his last humiliating defeat (which would conflict with verses 42-43). And he died in Persia, not in Israel (the land of the *"holy mountain"* mentioned in verse 45). All of these clues lead many scholars to suggest that Antiochus IV was almost like a scale model, or a foreshadowing, of a different king whose reign is prophesied beginning in Daniel 11:36. This king, some say, is the Antichrist.

- We looked into the Antichrist during our study of the little horn in Daniel 7 and *"the prince who is to come"* in Daniel 9:26. Read again the description of the Antichrist (*"man of lawlessness"*) in 2 Thessalonians 2:1-12. What similarities do you see between this passage and today's reading about the king of the north?

One of the defining characteristics of this king in Daniel 11:36 is that he will *"exalt himself and magnify himself above every god."* This evil ruler will believe he is god, or at least act like he believes he is god. This represents, in essence, a full-circle moment in the history of humanity — it sets a scene similar to the garden of Eden, where Satan tempted Eve with the forbidden fruit.

- In Genesis 3:5, the serpent specifically seduced her by saying, "*For God knows that when you eat of it your eyes will be opened, and you will ...*" what? In what ways does this describe the fundamental impulse of all sin?

Another characteristic of the evil king in Daniel 11 is that he will throw off *all* religions. He will only honor "*the god of fortresses*" (v. 38). The "*god of fortresses*" means war. War will be his religion. Fighting and conquering and bloodshed for the ultimate gain of more and more power will be what this king worships with "*gold and silver, with precious stones and costly gifts*" (v. 38). He will pour money, time, energy and thought into making war and gaining power.

- Matthew 6:21 says, "*For where your treasure is, there your heart will be also.*" What do you see yourself pouring your money, time, energy and thoughts into? How can this be an effective heart check against worshipping any other "gods" besides the one true God?

Daniel 11:40-45 gives us a glimpse into what will take place "*at the time of the end.*" These images are not so much precise details as they are events expressed in terms familiar to Daniel's day and time. From this account, we can conclude that the evil king will advance on and through other countries. There will be an invasion of Israel ("*the glorious land*" in verse 41). The world will be on the verge of complete conquest under this ruler. But he will become afraid (v. 44), and in anger, he will pour out destruction on his enemies. However, Daniel 11 ends with this sentence: "*Yet he shall come to his end, with none to help him*" (v. 45).

- This evil king is frightening — yet his end is summed up in one short sentence. What do you think this means about his power compared to God's power? How does this give you confidence that God is at work even when the world seems frightening?

In his commentary on Daniel, Daniel Akin provides a chart contrasting the Antichrist and King Jesus.[1] It is a beautiful and compelling reminder of the God we serve. We've excerpted a small portion of it here:

ANTIOCHUS/ANTICHRIST	KING JESUS
Willful (Daniel 11:36)	Submissive (Matthew 11:29)
Exalts himself (Daniel 11:36)	Humbles Himself (Philippians 2:8)
Magnifies himself as a god although he is *only human* (Daniel 11:36)	God incarnate: He is *God and human* at the same time (John 1:14)
Blasphemes God (Daniel 11:36)	Glorifies God (John 7:18)
Worships the god of war (Daniel 11:38)	Is the God of peace (Isaiah 9:6)
His kingdom will end (Daniel 11:45)	His Kingdom endures forever (Isaiah 9:7)

- What sticks out to you in these differences between Christ and the Antichrist? Let's close today by praising God for His goodness.

DANIEL 12:1-4
The vision ended with a look at the devastation and resurrection to come.

DAY 29

It is not easy or comfortable to talk about death — yet death is one of the things we all have to wrestle with. Similarly, it's not necessarily "fun" to think about end times — yet praise be to God that as followers of Jesus, we have a hope and future that neither death nor end times can take from us!

In today's reading, we'll find the conclusion of Daniel's vision of *"the end"* (v. 4). Let's begin with a look at the second sentence of Daniel 12:1: *"And there shall be a time of trouble, such as never has been since there was a nation till that time."*

The book of Daniel so far has been filled with evil rulers and resulting persecutions. We saw them personally in Daniel's own life. We saw prophecies that more evil kings would come for the Jewish people in the days of Antiochus IV. And the book of Daniel ends by saying the worst is actually yet to come. Jesus echoes this idea in Mark 13:19: *"For in those days there will be such tribulation as has not been from the beginning of the creation that God created until now, and never will be."* In the last days, the enemy of God will throw everything he has into stopping the people of God.

The good news is that we *"shall be delivered, everyone whose name shall be found written in [God's] book"* (Daniel 12:1). Various scholars and church denominations differ in their interpretations of whether this means God will deliver His people to heaven *before* the *"time of trouble"* on earth or *after* some or all the trouble, but we can all agree on the main truth: God will come through for us.

- How might studying the persecution and deliverance of others in the Bible — like Daniel, Stephen (Acts 7:54-60) or Paul (Acts 14:19-23), just to name a few — strengthen and steady us for the days to come?

Dark days are coming. But God also gives us assurances that will help us through this time.

Daniel 12:1 says that in the end, "*Michael, the great prince who has charge of [Daniel's] people,*" shall arise. Michael is the archangel thought to be a guardian of the people of Israel. And for believers in Jesus, Romans 11:17 says whether or not we are Jewish by birth, we are "*grafted in*" to Israel by faith and are inheritors of God's promises to His people. This means **the angels of God are on our side**. Bible scholar Dale Davis says, "There are unseen legions (cf. Matthew 26:53, Hebrews 1:14) standing behind the wobbly people of God in their darkest trouble."[1] We will not be left to fight any battle alone.

Daniel 12:1 also says **God's people are promised deliverance.** If your name is in God's book, it is sealed. Eternal life is yours, and nothing — *nothing* — can take you from God's hand (John 10:29). God will rescue those who are His.

- What else do Malachi 3:16, Luke 10:20 and Revelation 20:12 teach us about God's book? How does this give you confidence to face the future?

Daniel 12:2-3 then mentions the final resurrection. All people will resurrect, but sadly, some will resurrect to *"everlasting contempt"* (v. 2). Our hope is not simply in resurrection alone; our hope is that we will rise to *"everlasting life"* (v. 2). And the empty tomb of Jesus is the guarantee of **eternal life for all who believe in Him.**

- Knowing the promise of resurrection gives us an eternal perspective. Why do you think it's important to keep an eternal perspective as we walk through life?

Daniel 12:3 speaks of those who are wise and who turn others toward righteousness. We gain wisdom from God (Proverbs 2:6) through the study of His Word and time spent with Him in prayer. And through godly wisdom, we are then able to help, guide and encourage others. When hard times come, **we will need to be wise and strong for each other.**

- What is one way you can encourage someone you know who is going through a difficult time? Why is it important to use wisdom in deciding how to do this?

Daniel 12:4 ends with the angel telling Daniel to *"shut up the words and seal the book."* This was not a command to hide but rather to preserve and authenticate the visions Daniel had received. The Lord knew future generations would need to read these words to gain knowledge and stamina for remaining faithful to the end.

- End today by thanking God for preserving these words for you, and pray for wisdom and confidence in God's eternal plan for your life.

DAY 30

DANIEL 12:5-13
Daniel was told that the end would come and that, until then, he should go his way.

If you knew the end of this world was coming … what would you do? What *should* you do?

Today we end the book of Daniel by appropriately taking one last look at the end of time. As his final vision concluded, Daniel was left with an encouraging command that we can also take and apply to our lives "*till the end*" (Daniel 12:13).

In his vision, Daniel saw two angels, each standing on opposite banks of a stream. In the middle was the "*man clothed in linen,*" presumably the same one from Daniel 10:5 (who some scholars think was a pre-incarnate Christ). The angels asked Him an important question: "*How long shall it be till the end of these wonders?*" (Daniel 12:6).

- Do you ever find yourself wishing to know when the end of time will occur? Why or why not?

Even the angels have an interest in when the end shall come — yet as Jesus later said in Mark 13:32, "*Concerning that day or that hour, no one knows, not even the angels in heaven.*" So in Daniel 12:6, they did not get an exact timeline. Instead, their question was answered with two phrases:

1. "*A time, times, and half a time*" (v. 7). Scholars say this either means 3.5 "times" or simply a definite amount of time in the future.

2. "*When the shattering of the power of the holy people comes to an end*" (v. 7). This means when evil has done its worst and all hope for God's people seems gone.

After all this communication between angels and God, Daniel stated a most honest reply: "*I heard, but I did not understand*" (Daniel 12:8).

- In what ways are Daniel's words here comforting or encouraging to you as we end our study? How did the angelic beings assure Daniel in verse 9 despite his lack of understanding?

Just because Daniel did not understand doesn't mean he did not try. He kept asking good questions. And he was told that ultimately *"those who are wise shall understand"* (v. 10). It is possible that in the last days, the Lord's people will be given special understanding, and perhaps even these visions and revelations in Daniel will make more sense then. As Bible scholar James Boice says, there are things here "which we cannot yet explain."[1] The key word is "yet."

- We have learned through our study of Daniel that prophecy often holds meanings for the present day and future days. It would then make sense that there are some prophecies in the Bible we cannot understand until that time is revealed. How does knowing this help you appreciate the depth and complexity of God's Word? How do you see His power at work in the timeliness of His Word?

Most scholars admit not understanding the exact meaning of the numbers in Daniel 12:11-12. If we count them literally, 1,290 days translates to a little over 3.5 years. Then 1,335 days is 45 days longer. There does not seem to be any special symbolism surrounding this number. What we do know is there will be a set time when evil will do its absolute worst. And there will be people of God who endure. In fact, it seems they will still be standing after that evil time (v. 12). In the words of Bible scholar Dale Davis, "After evil does its worst, the church of Jesus will be there ... standing on their feet ... God is going to have a thirteen-thirty-five people."[2]

- How can you resolve to be a "thirteen-thirty-five" person: someone who will be found standing firm in Jesus long past everything this world attempts to throw at you?

We do not know if the end of days will happen in our lifetime or in years to come. But the word for us now is the same as it was for Daniel: "*Go your way till the end. And you shall rest and shall stand in your allotted place at the end of the days*" (Daniel 12:13).

For now, we keep living faithfully right where God has placed us. We will someday rest in death, but we also have the promise of resurrection. And, friend, if you trust in Christ, there is a place in eternity allotted for you. It will be your front-row seat to watch God's power working, His perfect plan unfolding, for all eternity.

- Try inserting your name in place of Daniel's in Daniel 12:9. How will you walk away from this study with confidence in God's power at work?

WEEKEND REFLECTION *and* PRAYER

Let's take a look at where we saw God's power at work in this final week's study:

First, Daniel saw a vision of kings from the south and north, and God's power was undeniable as we walked through history and saw the prophecies fulfilled (Daniel 11).

These kings from the south and north would continue in wickedness, but God declared everything had an "*appointed time*" (Daniel 11:35).

Even the worst ruler of all time will be no match for God. When God decides it's time, that person will "*come to his end*" (Daniel 11:45).

God showed that His power both *has* and *will have* the ability to rescue, resurrect and deliver into eternity those who are His (Daniel 12:1-3).

And while the end will be hard, by the power of God, the Church of Jesus will endure through anything and everything that comes its way (Daniel 12:12-13).

In seeing God's prophecies perfectly fulfilled, we find confidence in Him. We can learn to trust His appointed time for all things, knowing even evil and hard things must follow His timetable. We don't have to be afraid because we know our future is secure in Him. His Kingdom will endure to the end. We can stand on the words of Jesus: "*I will build my church, and the gates of hell shall not prevail against it*" (Matthew 16:18).

> *Father God, give us confidence in Your power at work. Every word You say has, does and will come true. We believe everything is subject to Your appointed timing. We believe in the security of our eternal life and home with You. We stand today, and every day, on the promise that Your Church will always endure no matter what is up ahead. Your power will make it so. We believe. In Jesus' name, amen.*

NOTES

NOTES

Endnotes

THE BABYLONIAN EMPIRE

[1] "Babylonia: Ancient Region, Mesopotamia." *Encyclopedia Britannica*, January 4, 2024. https://www.britannica.com/place/Babylonia.

[2] "Babylon." History.com, May 31, 2023. https://www.history.com/topics/ancient-middle-east/babylon.

THEMES AND PURPOSE OF DANIEL

[1] Davis, Dale Ralph. *The Message of Daniel*. The Bible Speaks Today, edited by J.A. Motyer. Downers Grove, IL: InterVarsity Press, 2013, p. 26.

DAY 1

[1] Davis, Dale Ralph. *The Message of Daniel*. The Bible Speaks Today, edited by J.A. Motyer. Downers Grove, IL: InterVarsity Press, 2013, p. 36.

DAY 3

[1] Pierce, Ronald W. *Daniel*. Teach the Text Commentary Series, Grand Rapids, MI: Baker Books, a division of Baker Publishing Group, 2015, p. 29.

DAY 4

[1] Akin, Daniel L. *Exalting Jesus in Daniel*. Christ-Centered Exposition, edited by David Platt, Daniel L. Akin, and Tony Merida, Nashville, TN: B&H Publishing Group, 2017, p. 21.

DAY 5

[1] Davis, Dale Ralph. *The Message of Daniel*. The Bible Speaks Today, edited by J.A. Motyer, Downers Grove, IL: InterVarsity Press, 2013, p. 46.

[2] Jeremiah, David. Quoted in Daniel L. Akin. *Exalting Jesus in Daniel*. Christ-Centered Exposition, edited by David Platt, Daniel L. Akin, and Tony Merida, Nashville, TN: B&H Publishing Group, 2017, p. 23.

DAY 6

[1] Henry, Matthew. *Matthew Henry's Commentary on the Whole Bible: Complete and Unabridged in One Volume*. Peabody: Hendrickson, 1994, p. 1433.

DAY 7

[1] "*Maliciously accused,*" Daniel 3:8. StepBible.org. https://www.stepbible.org/?q=version=ESV|reference=Dan.3&options=VHNUG&sort=false&pos=1.

DAY 8

[1] Pierce, Ronald W. *Daniel*. Teach the Text Commentary Series, Grand Rapids, MI: Baker Books, a division of Baker Publishing Group, 2015, pp. 64-65.

DAY 10

[1] Wolgemuth, Nancy DeMoss. "Heaven Rules." *Revive Our Hearts*, December 6, 2021. https://www.reviveourhearts.com/devotional/heaven-rules/.

DAY 11

[1] Spurgeon, Charles H. "Micah's Message for Today," 1889. Quoted in Daniel L. Akin. *Exalting Jesus in Daniel*. Christ-Centered Exposition, edited by David Platt, Daniel L. Akin, and Tony Merida, Nashville, TN: B&H Publishing Group, 2017, p. 49.

DAY 12

[1] Davis, Dale Ralph. *The Message of Daniel*. The Bible Speaks Today, edited by J.A. Motyer, Downers Grove, IL: InterVarsity Press, 2013, p. 74.

[2] Pierce, Ronald W. *Daniel*. Teach the Text Commentary Series, Grand Rapids, MI: Baker Books, a division of Baker Publishing Group, 2015, p. 91.

DAY 13

[1] Santayana, George. *The Life of Reason Vol. 1: Reason in Common Sense*. London Constable, London, 1905.

[2] Davis, Dale Ralph. *The Message of Daniel*. The Bible Speaks Today, edited by J.A. Motyer, Downers Grove, IL: InterVarsity Press, 2013, p. 80.

DAY 14

[1] Davis, Dale Ralph. *The Message of Daniel*. The Bible Speaks Today, edited by J.A. Motyer, Downers Grove, IL: InterVarsity Press, 2013, p. 82.

DAY 15

[1] Akin, Daniel L. *Exalting Jesus in Daniel*. Christ-Centered Exposition, edited by David Platt, Daniel L. Akin, and Tony Merida, Nashville, TN: B&H Publishing Group, 2017, p. 73.

[2] Matthews, Victor Harold, Mark W. Chavalas and John H. Walton. "Daniel 6:8," *The IVP Bible Background Commentary: Old Testament*. Downers Grove, IL: InterVarsity Press, 2000.

APOCALYPTIC LITERATURE

[1] "Apocalyptic Literature." *How to Read the Bible Series,* BibleProject, June 9, 2020. https://bibleproject.com/explore/video/apocalyptic-literature/?gclid=CjwKCAjw6eWnBhAKEiwADpnw9l70IiolbN9lFr4s4YoroEpYkFLgHDpmVpwUsC8Fl0CPfmXUe6rT_RoCTE0QAvD_BwE.

WHAT DID THE BEASTS OF DANIEL 7 REPRESENT?

[1] *The ESV Study Bible*. Wheaton, IL: Crossway, 2008, pp. 1599-1600.

DAY 19

[1] Ferguson, Sinclair B. "Daniel," *The Preacher's Commentary*, vol. 21. Nashville, TN: Thomas Nelson, 1988, pp. 147-148.

DAY 21

[1] Davis, Dale Ralph. *The Message of Daniel*. The Bible Speaks Today, edited by J.A. Motyer, Downers Grove, IL: InterVarsity Press, 2013, p. 111.

[2] "2 Maccabees 9:5-7." Quoted in Daniel L. Akin. *Exalting Jesus in Daniel*. Christ-Centered Exposition, edited by David Platt, Daniel L. Akin, and Tony Merida, Nashville, TN: B&H Publishing Group, 2017, p. 104.

DAY 22

[1] Baldwin, Joyce G. *Daniel: An Introduction and Commentary*, vol. 23. Tyndale Old Testament Commentaries, Downers Grove, IL: InterVarsity Press, 1978, p. 183.

[2] Veldkamp, Herman. *Dreams and Dictators*. St. Catharines: Paideia, 1978, p. 202. Quoted in Davis, Dale Ralph. *The Message of Daniel*. The Bible Speaks Today, edited by J.A. Motyer, Downers Grove, IL: InterVarsity Press, 2013, p. 119.

DAY 24

[1] Duncan, Ligon. "The Vision of the Man." Sermon, March 15, 1998. http://ligonduncan.com/the-vision-of-the-man-875.

DAY 25

[1] Piper, John. "Angels and Prayer." Sermon, January 12, 1992. http://www.desiringgod.org/messages/angels-and-prayer.

[2] Miller, Stephen R. *Daniel: The New American Commentary*, vol. 18. Nashville, TN: B&H, 1994, p. 285.

KINGS OF THE SOUTH (PTOLEMAIC EMPIRE)

[1] *The ESV Study Bible*. Wheaton, IL: Crossway, 2008, pp. 1610-1616.

KINGS OF THE NORTH (SELEUCID EMPIRE)

[1] *The ESV Study Bible*. Wheaton, IL: Crossway, 2008, pp. 1610-1616.

DAY 28

[1] Akin, Daniel L. *Exalting Jesus in Daniel*. Christ-Centered Exposition, edited by David Platt, Daniel L. Akin, and Tony Merida, Nashville, TN: B&H Publishing Group, 2017, p. 157.

DAY 29

[1] Davis, Dale Ralph. *The Message of Daniel*. The Bible Speaks Today, edited by J.A. Motyer, Downers Grove, IL: InterVarsity Press, 2013, p. 162.

DAY 30

[1] Boice, James Montgomery. *Daniel: An Expositional Commentary*. Grand Rapids, MI: Baker, 2003, p. 122.

[2] Davis, Dale Ralph. *The Message of Daniel*. The Bible Speaks Today, edited by J.A. Motyer, Downers Grove, IL: InterVarsity Press, 2013, p. 168.

ABOUT *Proverbs 31* MINISTRIES

*She is clothed with strength and dignity;
she can laugh at the days to come.*
PROVERBS 31:25

Proverbs 31 Ministries is a nondenominational, nonprofit Christian ministry that seeks to lead women into a personal relationship with Christ. With Proverbs 31:10-31 as a guide, Proverbs 31 Ministries reaches women in the middle of their busy days through free devotions, podcast episodes, speaking events, conferences, resources, and training in the call to write, speak and lead others.

We are real women offering real-life solutions to those striving to maintain life's balance, in spite of today's hectic pace and cultural pull away from godly principles.

Wherever a woman may be on her spiritual journey, Proverbs 31 Ministries exists to be a trusted friend who understands the challenges she faces and walks by her side, encouraging her as she walks toward the heart of God.

Visit us online today at proverbs31.org!

P31 PROVERBS 31 ministries

Like Daniel lived as an exile in Babylon, we, too, are living as exiles in a foreign land.

Learn more in our newest study ...

WHERE DO I BELONG?

Finding Our True Home Through the Study of Exile in the Bible

Available September 2024 at p31bookstore.com.